THE B.O.W.S.

THE
B.O.W.S.

By MARGALO GILLMORE
and PATRICIA COLLINGE

HARCOURT, BRACE AND COMPANY
NEW YORK

DEDICATED TO UNIT 319
AND THE MEN IT PLAYED TO

FOREWORD

In case anyone should be confused by the fact that this book has two authors and yet is written in the first person singular, this is to beg him not to give it another thought. Margalo Gillmore went overseas with *The Barretts of Wimpole Street* and it is she who tells the story of her journey. I have been no nearer to NATOUSA and ETOUSA than the postmarks on Margalo's letters to me, letters which were the beginning of our collaboration.

I don't know whether one collaborator can dedicate his part of the work to the other; but if he can, my contribution is dedicated to Margalo Gillmore in gratitude for having let me share, through working with her, in all the things that had so stirred and moved her; and for letting me be, however vicariously, part of an adventure that I could not otherwise have experienced.

PATRICIA COLLINGE

THE B.O.W.S.

CHAPTER ONE

IT BEGAN with the telephone.

I don't suppose the operator who put through that first call to Philadelphia had any idea that it was more than the usual routine person-to-person, hold-the-wire, please, I-will-connect-you transaction, but to us at the other end it was pretty momentous. Though even then I am not sure that we were completely aware of all that connection was going to mean.

It had seemed simple enough to ask Katharine Cornell if she would head a company to go overseas. Maybe she would, maybe she wouldn't; we couldn't tell till we asked her, could we?

And I felt we should do that. "We could write her a letter," I said to Bert Lytell and Antoinette Perry that day in the office of the American Theatre Wing. "Or one of us could go over to Philadelphia and see her."

"We could call her right up," said Tony Perry and reached for the telephone.

It was hot in the office, and the clock on Tiffany's across the street stood at five, as the three of us sat waiting for the call to be completed. I remember looking out of the window, but instead of Fifth Avenue I saw a theater dressing room in Philadelphia, and Katharine Cornell just back there after the matinee, with no thought beyond a shower and some food and a rest before the evening performance. I could almost hear the telephone ring there, and see her reach casually for it with no suspicion that she was about to change the whole course of her life, and I wished that I could send her a telepathic warning. I also wished that someone would invent a gadget for telephones that would show a red light or send up a rocket or at least yell "Watch yourself!" when some out-of-the-ordinary news was on the way. It's not fair, I thought; here we sit knowing all about it, and there she is, innocently reaching for a bombshell. We should

3

have written to her first, I thought, we should have gone over to see her, we should have . . .

But she must have answered at that very second, because Tony Perry was talking, and going straight to the point. Other units had gone overseas for the USO but this was to be a project of the American Theatre Wing. Would Miss Cornell undertake to head it, choosing her own play and company?

I thought I heard a soft sound that might have been a gasp. "Will you talk to Bert, now?" said Tony, and Bert Lytell, president of the Actor's Equity Association, took over and after a few brief sentences I heard my name.

"Margalo Gillmore is backing us up," he said, smiling, and handed me the telephone.

I couldn't say much more than that I hoped she would do it. "It's a bit of a surprise," she said.

"I know it is," I said. "But, darling Kit, forgive us for springing it at you, and think about it."

I hung up.

"Well?" we all asked each other at once.

"She didn't say no," said Bert. "She is going to think it over and let us know tomorrow. Of course, she has a lot of commitments; she would have to cancel her tour . . ."

He looked at me. "What do you think, Margalo?" he asked. "Will she do it?"

"I don't know," I said. But I thought I did.

And the next day she called up and said yes. "I *wanted* to say it yesterday," she said, "but I had to catch my breath."

And that was that. Kit had said yes, and I knew we were as good as there. There were a few preliminaries, of course, before we actually landed on the other side, or even started for it. First, the play had to be decided on. Kit considered for a while and then said she would like to take *The Barretts of Wimpole Street*, if Brian Aherne would play Robert Browning as he had in her original production of the Rudolph Besier play. So Brian was asked and he said certainly he would. McKay Morris joined up to play Edward Moulton-Barrett, the terrifying father of the Wimpole Street family, and Brenda Forbes took over her old part of Wilson, Elizabeth Barrett's faithful maid.

I don't suppose there is anyone who doesn't know that Katharine Cornell is married to Guthrie McClintic, the producer and director. Guthrie directs all Kit's plays, and for our tour reverted to acting, to play one of Miss Barrett's doctors, and there were Emily Lawrence, Betty Brewer, Chester Stratton, Erik Martin, Keinert Wolff, Robert Ross and me. Robert is my husband, and he and Guthrie ran each other neck and neck in excitement and enthusiasm. We were all of us excited if it came to that, but Bob and Guthrie made us look torpid in comparison.

It was their idea that we should have something up our sleeves to do at hospitals where we couldn't give the play. Maybe a little revue. We already had Brenda Forbes who could give one all by herself if pressed. Betty Brewer could sing and Erik Martin could dance. The idea grew and expanded. Roger Stearns came along to play in the play, but primarily to make his piano the prop and backbone of the Barrett's musical moments.

"What about songs and sketches?" asked Bob avidly. So we gained Nancy Hamilton as lyricist and teammate to Brenda's comedy, and Tony Perry's daughter Elaine to combine a bit of serious singing with a touch of glamour.

The technical department consisted officially of Bill Noon— Irish, stocky, stoical, and a demon electrician. The prospect of lighting overseas stages with overseas equipment had no terror for him, used though he was to the lavish paraphernalia of New York theaters. But he did wonder if he would be able to take enough cigars with him to last the trip.

"I should think so," said Guthrie. "Do you smoke many?"

"About twenty-five a day," said Bill.

"I guess you'd better talk to Miss Macy," said Guthrie.

Miss Macy was Gert Macy who is Kit's personal manager. She was coming with us in that capacity and almost every other. If anything could be procured, Gert would procure it, and if anything couldn't be done, Gert would do it, so she very likely took over the problem of Bill's cigars, just as she later took over all our problems on the trip, including being our stage manager and giving intrepid aid to Nancy Hamilton who was doubling as wardrobe mistress. Everyone took on whatever extra work he could. The men of the cast were to help set the stage. Elaine

Perry would be assistant stage manager for Gert, and my husband Bob added our financial management to his assignment of playing two parts with what he hoped would be totally different characterizations.

That was the cast and crew of the Barretts that was to become Unit 319.

In the meantime, the Wing with the Army and the USO had been very busy indeed. The production of the Barretts was to be on a much larger scale than any other unit that had been sent overseas. These first units had been planned to play in camps and hospitals or anywhere there was room to stand up. The plays were cut to an hour's length, and the equipment curtailed in proportion. We were to play in theaters, and we were to be allowed five thousand pounds of scenery and equipment as against the usual restriction of five hundred, and we would be seventeen people instead of the regulation seven. The play was to be played in its entirety, and the production was to suggest, as far as possible, the sense and illusion of the complete theater.

And everyone was enthusiastic and everyone agreed to everything until the USO found out about the play and then doubts began to set in. *The Barretts of Wimpole Street?* Wasn't that the play about Elizabeth Barrett and Robert Browning? But weren't they poets? We said they had been. And weren't they, well . . . not very young poets?

We said, strictly speaking, they were not exactly adolescent. And wasn't it a costume play, long skirts and things? We said it was.

Oh, dear, said the USO. Oh, dear, dear, dear. They said a great deal more than that but the general sense of it was that that was no play to give the troops. The men wouldn't like a play about poets, they said, but if they did they wouldn't like a play about middle-aged poets. They wouldn't like a play about middle-aged *anythings.* The men wanted pretty girls and lots of laughs. They wouldn't even *go* to a play like the Barretts, but if they did they would just walk out again, and if they didn't walk out, they would stay only to laugh us off the stage. There was a good deal of head shaking and arid gloom.

Kit listened to our reports of this.

"I don't know," she said. "I want to do my best for them, and this is the best I have to do."

She seemed to go deep into herself while she thought over the various dismal predictions.

Then she sat up rather straight.

"If they're not going to like it, then they're not going to like it, but it's the best I know how to do for them. We'll let them decide."

So we went into rehearsal and came head-on to another problem. What were we going to do about Flush, Elizabeth Barrett's famous spaniel? In the original production Flush was played by a dignified cocker, who rose to prominence by reason of an unshakeable calm in the face of his public, a calm so deep as to suggest profound slumber, so that at times small muttering groups formed to report that he was either stuffed or drugged or both. But he was neither; he was a normal healthy dog, and lived through the entire run of the play, until, after a period of retirement, which pleasantly included fatherhood, he died. But even if he had endured, he could not have joined us in his old place, because cocker spaniels weigh too much, and already we had our full quota of weight. A pound or two more was all that the budget, the Army, and the USO would allow.

So we tried a toy dog. It came from Mr. Schwarz's and it was every inch a phony, and it lasted one rehearsal. We might have got used to it, in spite of the fact that every time Brenda Forbes handled this monster we broke into wails and giggles, and in some cases, small screams; we might have attempted the impossible, we might have sailed with a white plush sepulcher had it not been for the moment when Kit herself held it aloft.

"Oh, you're coming with us, too, Flush; we're going to see Rome together," she said, addressing it in the words of Elizabeth Barrett. She gazed into its black button-eyes and shuddered.

"But I don't think you are," she added in her own person, and tossed it permanently aside.

This cheered us, and we cheered Kit, but it left us still without Flush, until the day a small Yorkshire terrier came into our lives and our hearts. He was tiny, exquisite, and looked as delicate as air, though he was to prove himself a lion in endurance.

He examined us quietly, weighed us, and made straight for Brenda Forbes and waved a golden paw in surrender. It was love at first sight for them; from then on they were inseparable, and at our first abandon-ship drill Brenda put him in the hood of her raincoat and tied it firmly under her chin.

"So he can lick my face as we climb down to the lifeboat," she explained.

But that came later. Lots of things happened to us before we got as far as boat drill. We didn't even know there would be such a thing, we didn't even know there would be a boat, we didn't know that when there was a boat we would learn to call it a ship. We didn't know, really, very much of anything. We had all, naturally, gone on long trips before, we had all toured, we had most of us been abroad, but that had been when it was still abroad, and not overseas, and we had had some standard on which to base our expectations. Now we had no smallest idea of where we were going, how we would get there, or what it would be like when we did. It was like going to sea without a compass, and finally, as the weeks passed, and we had gone through the stages of getting ready and reached the one of being ready, and passed from that to one of just waiting, it all suddenly became somehow unreal. We had our uniforms, but that we would wear them anywhere but Beekman Place (where most of us lived) ceased to be reasonable. We packed, we rehearsed, we disposed of our various apartments, we had a preliminary performance at Mitchel Field, but it seemed to have no connection with anything further. We retreated into a haze of suspended sleepiness, partly the result of the really terrific heat of that summer of 1944 and partly induced by the various inoculations permeating our unaccustomed systems. I gave up worrying about the reception of the Barretts overseas. If we were ever going to open officially, I decided, it would probably be in Boston.

Then one steamy afternoon, the telephone in our apartment rang. It had been ringing a good deal in this period of waiting, but we had long since stopped jumping for our musette bags when we heard it. I was lying on my bed, and I stayed there.

Bob answered, and then he came and stood looking down at me.

"Well," he said. "We're alerted. We're going."

For a minute I almost asked where, and then I sat up straight. We were going. We were going overseas. It wasn't something to be talked about any more, it was real.

I felt excited and elated and terrified. All sorts of things rushed into my mind. Our cat, George, would she miss us? My mother . . . why hadn't I seen her more, I should have spent every minute with her. I should have had the slipcovers cleaned. The apartment, when would I see it again? It was so comfortable and cool. I couldn't have been more wrong about that, but it seemed so for the moment. Would I have to fly? Would I be sick if I did? Would they really hate the Barretts?

I stared at Robert and tried to express some of all this to him.

"Oh," I said, a bit flatly.

And I called up my mother.

From then on, it was a sort of montage that never really came clear till we were on the ship. The telephone rang and rang. Kit called.

"Is it really real?" she said.

People came to say good-bye. We packed in earnest, and it got steadily hotter. There were last cocktails. We went down in the elevator wondering when we would be brought up again. And then it was eleven o'clock of an August night, and we were at a station in our winter uniforms getting a first taste of the reality of sweating it out. We looked nice, though, I thought. All of us. Very neat and pressed, even if we didn't feel it.

Kit clutched my hand.

"Why are we doing it?" she whispered, in a last moment panic.

Well, we were going to find out.

We looked at our luggage, mysteriously initialed I.J.142-YE. What did that mean?

We were going to find that out, too.

CHAPTER TWO

OUR FIRST step on the way to finding out was taken when, late the next day, we were led from the train to an army post and our introduction to army post life.

It was still hot, and our uniforms were no cooler than they had been the night before.

"It'll be sure to be cool at the post," we told each other comfortingly. "Barracks, you know. Those big buildings are always cool."

Maybe they are, but the big buildings turned out, for the distaff side at any rate, to be a structure of tar-paper with a tin roof that held every last ray of the sun in which it had been baking all day. There was a stretch of thirty beds, twenty-two of which were occupied by sleeping, perspiring WACS. We were perspiring, too, but I for one didn't feel I was going to do much sleeping, and the sight of a large iron stove with a basket of kindling right beside my cot didn't help me to feel any cooler. This is probably heaven compared to what our men have, we thought, which buoyed us considerably until we found out later that evening that the boys had been luxuriously billeted in the officers' quarters.

The next four days began at six in the morning and ended at six at night, with an abandoned amount of activity in between. We had all been fingerprinted, and had had our pictures taken, but we did it all over again, and attended lectures as well. And our focus was trained, not on whether the Barretts would be a success or a failure, but on the possibility and the emergency of collective and individual death.

We had our gas masks fitted and wore them for ten minutes in a lethal chamber where Nancy's leaked and she had to be let out, her eyes streaming but her spirit undampened. And we had abandon-ship drill. We were taken to an open space where there was a high structure rigged to the approximate height and angle of a sinking ship. It was draped with a sinister net of heavy rope, and all we had to do, they explained kindly, was climb the ladder at the back of this stock-company vessel and then climb down the rope ladder net to a property lifeboat which waited apathetically at its foot. Brian, Gert and I took one look at this contraption, and, since scaling it was not compulsory, declined. Brian had a lame knee, and I am a sissy about height, and decided I would do better in the inspiration of a real emergency. Gert refused for some strong reason which I don't remember now, but I think she had some idea of standing by and catching the cast as they fell one by one. I often try to imagine parents with sufficient character to have produced Gert, and end up by seeing them as a combination of the lion of Trafalgar Square and the one in front of the New York Public Library.

Now Gert took a sturdy stance below as the rest of the Barretts went valiantly up and down. Betty Brewer was the first to tackle it, and I remembered that she had been the first in the gas chamber. She is a small girl, but Flush was her only equal in pluck in proportion to size. Brenda came gaily, with Flush triumphant in the hood of her raincoat. Kit came with steady concentration, like a Juliet abandoning her balcony. Guthrie as captain of our unit, if not of a ship, came last, looking very noble but giving a vague impression of a fly caught on a piece of flypaper. Kit called to him from the ground, where she was watching in critical apprehension, that he had started with the wrong foot.

"Don't direct me *now*, baby, or I'll never get untangled," he yelled back, and continued his descent.

And as he landed in safety we burst into song:

> With his bell-bottom trousers
> And his coat of navy blue
> Climbing down the riggin'
> As his Daddy used to do.*

That day happened to be his birthday, and we sang it again to him when we celebrated it that night. He was served a large

* By special permission of copyright owner, Santly-Joy, Inc. Copyright, 1944.

birthday cake baked by one of the Italian prisoners of war, whom
we were learning to call co-belligerents. We toasted Guthrie,
and he said in reply that it was the happiest birthday of his life
—a statement we thoroughly understood and subscribed to, because in a way it was our birthday too, and the future was a
present that we hadn't unwrapped. We had no idea what was
lurking inside, but the outside fascinated us. Our guesses as to
the contents were not helped much by our first contact with
scuttlebutt, the service's generic term for rumor. Some thought
we might stay at the post for weeks. Lots of people had, they
said darkly. Four girls in our barracks had lost their passports
and were being sent back to New York, and their constant tears
did little to enliven our surroundings. We were about to break
into a few frustrated sobs ourselves when the government came
through and presented us each with a tin of insecticide, a steel
helmet, a webbed belt, and a canteen, all of which we were expected to carry along with our recently acquired gas masks and
our now familiar musette bags. Kit took a look at the collection
and called a rehearsal that evening to see if we could possibly get
it all on, and somehow we did. It weighed a bit, but our hearts
were much lighter, because something told us we wouldn't be
given all those things just for the hell of it.

That something was right. The next morning men came in and
stamped all our luggage, and we were told to pick up our pass-
port and AGO cards, which were our identification cards giving
us the rank of captains or, as the Army has it, assimilated captains, so if we were taken prisoner we would be treated as such.
We also got our dog-tags, and Flush, to Brenda's satisfaction,
got one, too.

Then came the moment we had been waiting for. They told us
that when we got our passports we would find our destination
printed on them. Trembling with eagerness we looked, and there
it was:

Natousa. North African Theatre of United States Army.

We had a destination, now, and we were on our way to it.

We got our equipment on, and waited for the bus that was
to pick us up that afternoon at four, to take us to the train that
would take us to the boat. While we waited we practiced "about

face" which we had been told we would have to do on the march to the train with the soldiers. If we were going to march with soldiers, we weren't going to let them down, so we about faced till we could do it without falling over ourselves and each other. When we got that down more or less pat, we went on to practicing saluting, as the colonel of the post had told us that he would salute us as we marched past, and he expected us to return it in good form.

The bus came. My heart beat fast as I got on, but no more than the others'. We rode past company after company of men sweating under their steel helmets as they waited with their packs on their backs. As we passed they cheered us. We wanted to cheer back, but we couldn't have made a sound. At least I know I couldn't. I might have tried but I was too excited and moved to have achieved anything more than a hiccup. We got to the train and got off the bus. A band was playing, and more companies of men were waiting. The men spied Betty Brewer, the baby of the company.

"Hey! Come on and dance," they called and in a minute she was jitterbugging with them, her canteen flying, her gas mask flopping.

She was a beautiful dancer, and elfinly pretty, and spirits soared just looking at her. The immediacy of departure was forgotten in that small gay moment and the troops took Betty over and she lost her last name, and remained forever just Betty to the thousands of men who were going on that trip with us and for one in particular that we didn't know about yet.

Things blurred for me a bit then; there was movement and confusion and then sudden order. We were marching to the train. We got the word to about face and accomplished it beautifully. We applauded ourselves mentally and concentrated on keeping in step. The men of our group marched in front, we women behind mumbling, "Left, left—I had a good home but I *left*," to keep ourselves in step. We were doing ourselves and the Army and the USO and the Theatre Wing and our families proud till all of a sudden the men fell out of step and, cursing, we automatically followed them. But it was not till much later when we fell on them and asked furiously why they had betrayed us that we found out that Brian Aherne had been the cause. It seemed that he had been marching along quite happily till it came over him that he wasn't really a soldier and to try to behave like one was, well, not exactly cricket, so he stopped marching and strolled.

We knew exactly what he meant. In spite of our uniforms, we were still civilians, and for us to seem to be aping soldiers could be thought tasteless. Only a truly modest and sensitive person like Brian could have had such a reaction, and in our hearts we agreed with it, but we couldn't help wishing that he hadn't had it right in the middle of our marching. But we got to the train, and small things like being in or out of step faded as we pulled out.

The band played "Over There." I don't think anyone spoke. Kit's eyes were wet. I just kept thinking, "I'm American," over and over again, as if I could never say it enough. The train went faster and the music died away leaving us all silent, and then the airmen who were on the train with us made a curiously concerted movement. They all turned their faces to the window and looked out as if they were trying to see farther than sight, and as we watched them we reached out in our thoughts to all those they loved, and all who loved them, and then . . . a voice sang out, a true sweet Irish tenor voice—

> I've got sixpence, jolly, jolly sixpence,
> I've got sixpence to last me all my life.

One by one other voices joined in.

> I've got tuppence to lend and tuppence to spend
> And tuppence to send home to my wife . . . poor wife!
> No cares have I to grieve me
> No pretty little girls to deceive me,

On this line they all laughed and looked at Betty and Emily and Elaine, and the tension was gone and the song rolled on wholeheartedly:

> I'm happy as a king, believe me,
> As we go rolling, rolling home,
> Rolling home, rolling home
> By the light of the silvery mo—oo—oon.

> Happy is the day
> When the airman gets his pay
> As we go rolling, rolling home.

I will remember that song a long time, and I will also remember that when we reached the dock, the band there was giving a twentieth century emphasis to the late Victorian gusto of "Ta-ra-ra-boom-de-ay." The band was part of our send-off which was being done in style. Photographers were taking pictures of us. Red Cross women were giving us welcome cups of ice-cold lemonade and saying, "Good luck and safe return." Blue uniforms and white duffle bags mixed with the khaki to announce that we were being reinforced by the Navy. And loud-speakers were calling out the numbers for the various units to go aboard the ship.

As the soldiers passed us, with their heavy barracks bags over their shoulders, I noticed that some of them had coat hangers sticking out from them.

"That's what *you* should have brought," I said to myself.

"Unit IJ-142-YE," bawled the loud-speaker.

"Is that us?" we asked.

"Yes, that's us, go ahead," said Gert Macy.

Again the loud-speaker instructed us.

"Once aboard this ship you are sealed on, and no one is allowed to leave." It sounded very firm.

We were walking up the gangplank; I could feel it lift and fall slightly under my feet. I smelt the smell of ship and water, my stomach revolved slowly inside me, and the small tour from the land to the ship was over.

A brisk voice shouted our last names to which we were to answer with our first.

"McClintic."

"Guthrie," answered Guthrie.

"McClintic."

"Katharine," said a very small voice.

One of Kit's visual charms, it seems to me, is her delicate and heart-shaped face which, at times, has a way of seeming to grow very small. It was doing it now, till I feared we would be left to sail with nothing but a pair of enormous eyes. All our names were called; all were responded to—we were on board. Sealed aboard.

Bob asked me what had been my last thought as I left the land. I think he hoped that I would come through with some fine noble sentiment, something worth remembering in the years of our old age. I considered making something up, but I capitulated to truth.

"I wished I had brought a coat-hanger," I said.

And I wished it again when I got to our quarters which were in the isolation ward, just off the sick bay. It was very neat, white and medicinal, but it was going to be awfully crowded as four strangers had swelled our number to twelve. All twelve of us women, of course, as the males and the females were clinically segregated.

Gert took in our none too roomy cabin and swung into magnificent action. The four strangers were quickly put together in a corner to themselves and the rest of our berths assigned. Seeing we had only one shower Gert hastily made out a list of hours for us to use it, and apportioned it.

We were wondering what to do next, when the loud-speaker decided for us, as we were to find it would do daily, if not hourly. This time, it announced that there would be a meeting in the wardroom at eight-thirty, and that all officers and USO players were expected to attend.

So we thought we had better get our equipment distributed first, which was when we found we had no cupboard space of any kind and that we would have to hang our clothes on the sides of our berths. But before we could get on with even that unattractive bit of home-making, the loud-speaker was at it again.

"The meeting in the wardroom has been changed to eight o'clock," it said severely.

Insanely I found myself wanting to ask it why, but I refrained and decided to go and find Bob. But when I eventually found his cabin it was guarded by a marine with a forty-five on his hip, who told me that women were not allowed in the men's quarters.

"But it's not a *man* . . . it's my husband!" I exclaimed.

"I can't help *that*, ma'am," he replied reasonably. So I gave up and went to the wardroom to wait for the meeting and Bob.

I don't quite know what I expected a wardroom to look like, something rather official with lots of steel and maps, perhaps. Actually, it seemed like a room in a club; not a Union or Harvard Club, but a plain sort of club, for plain men with no exotic tastes or privileges. There were green baize tables, and plain sturdy chairs, and at one end was what we would find to be the PX, though it was closed now.

I wondered what the meeting would be like and what it was for. Last minute instructions? My mind went back to cruises I had taken in prewar days. Probably, I thought, it's a sort of first-night-out get-together meeting, a welcome to our new surroundings. I brightened as I formed a picture of a fatherly captain beaming at us as he wished us good-night and good sailing, and led us in "Auld Lang Syne." The wardroom was filling up, and as our own group assembled we drifted automatically together. Before the captain appeared we were approached by a drunken sergeant who was swaying from table to table.

"Watch your p's and q's," he warned us, " 'cause this ship's going to be run properly, and we won't stand for no drinking, and I mean it," said he menacingly, with a definite stagger.

We were about to assure him that we would be governed by his lightest word, when he pulled himself to a semblance of sober attention.

The meeting was on. But I had imagined it all wrong. The captain did not even appear. It was a colonel who addressed us, and he wished us neither good-night nor good anything else.

First he said nothing. He just stood and looked us over with an expression of fierce dissatisfaction. Then he called the roll. Twenty lieutenants failed to show up.

The colonel went a rich purple. He snatched his glasses from his nose, placed them on the table in front of him, and in a harsh voice unwittingly echoed the words of our sergeant friend.

"This ship is going to be disciplined, and I'm going to see to it." He paused and glared, and continued.

"Every man who did not appear at this meeting will report to me at nine tomorrow and go without his breakfast." And to emphasize breakfast he thumped his fist on the table, striking his glasses which broke into pieces. Anything after that would have been anti-climactic and I think he realized it, for he merely gave us one last glare and finished with a command.

"Now everyone will return to his quarters."

We retired, very much subdued, to the isolation ward for our first night aboard.

Oddly enough, in spite of the newness of our surroundings and the closeness of our cabin-mates, we slept fairly well, awaking to find ourselves weathering a hurricane. That took care of any further activity on my part for the next three days, but the hardier sailors of our group brought me news of the world outside. The ship was jammed, they said, the decks tightly packed with standing men. Brian had surveyed them and murmured plaintively: "What, no deck chairs?" The captain, it was rumored, far from the parental paragon I had imagined, should have been called Bligh. He was a woman hater and a dog destroyer; he had had three dogs killed on the last trip, dogs that the men had smuggled aboard in their musette bags. "I hope he understands," said Brenda, "that Flush is an actor."

Nancy had met the colonel of the broken glasses, who told her that the drunken sergeant had been dealt with sternly. He had also showed her a bowie knife which he said he always carried because if it was necessary to abandon ship, too many men might try to cling to one raft, and in that case it would be his duty to cut their hands off.

"Though that would only take care of one raft," said Nancy. "What would he do about the others? Swim from raft to raft with the knife in his teeth?"

Kit had gone on deck and had run right into a young man called Gordon Stansfield who came from Martha's Vineyard, the island where Kit normally spent her summer days. The minute she saw him, Kit said, the troopship shrank, and they might have been on the boat that goes from Woods Hole to the Vineyard, with the island in sight.

McKay Morris, everyone agreed, was riding the hurricane in happy triumph. Britannia may rule the waves for the Empire, but for USO Unit 319 it was McKay Morris. I reviled his strong stomach to myself in miserable envy, but I cheered a little when I found I was not the only sufferer aboard. The loud-speaker an-

nounced that there would be no service at meals, as the enlisted
men who had volunteered as waiters were too ill to attend to
their duties. It would be nice, the loud-speaker suggested, if volunteers could now be found to help tidy up the sick men's
quarters. Lavishly, Bob and Keinert Wolff rushed to represent
our group. Keinert lasted on the job for a while, at least, but
Bob got down three steps and staggered back into the open air.

Why didn't they use their gas masks, I wondered from my
heaving bed.

But the fourth day was sweet and gentle, as far as the ocean
went. Out on deck the men swayed slightly with the ship, as the
loud-speaker relentlessly hounded them with advice.

"Life preservers are to be worn at all times. Do not sit or lean
on your life preserver. Do not throw anything overboard; it
leaves a trail for submarines to pick up. No shorts are to be worn,
and the men must keep their shirts on. Do not lean on the rail—
any man falling overboard will not be picked up."

This last was always greeted with a round of applause.

It was hot, it was stifling; our portholes closed with the blackout at six. We were supposed to be out of our cabins from nine
to eleven in the mornings, but once out there was no place to sit
down, hardly any place to stand. We tried to find some way to
be comfortable, and I began to understand the restless movement
of an animal that goes round and round before it sits down, only
to get up again and repeat the process. In the mess hall Captain
Bligh would not allow the men and women to eat together, nor
were they allowed on the same deck together. Our only sanc-
tioned meeting-place was the wardroom, which was usually so
packed that while it made contact close, it had also to be pretty
impersonal. I thought a little peevishly of the people who had
said how wonderful it was that my husband and I were going together on this journey.

"Just think," they had exclaimed. "To have that wonderful experience, and be together, too!"

To be together *where*, I asked myself bitterly as I would try
to catch Bob's eye across barriers till we began to feel like flir-
tatious strangers. Sometimes we met on forbidden ground, but
before long a courteous MP would join us.

"You're on the wrong deck, sir," he would point out gently; but he meant, "Break it up, boys," and we did.

The colonel met us each morning with a word of fright.

"I suppose you're glad the hurricane is over," he said, my first morning up. "Shouldn't be. This is the worst possible weather for subs. Better sleep with your clothes on tonight."

Fast though it was, at times the ship seemed slow enough. The long days rolled out in a repeated pattern of meals, lifeboat drills, and target practice when the ships' guns fired for half an hour and an acrid smell of powder would permeate the isolation ward where we women were confined till it was over. Hating the noise of the guns, I usually retired with two pillows over my head, trying to shut it out. But the powder smell penetrated, and lingered for all of us, reminding us that our ship was a stern one, bent only on fulfilling its great and terrible purpose of carrying men to war.

It was at times like this that Kit was very still, wondering if we were going to justify our coming. She was not worrying about the reception of the Barretts; it went much deeper than that with her. It was our being there at all. Seventeen actors against seventeen soldiers who might have been in our places. Five thousand pounds of scenery taking the space of five thousand pounds of equipment. Our usefulness seemed debatable in the face of the needs of a fighting world.

The colonel did nothing to reassure us.

"What's that thing you're going over to do, some sort of show, is it?"

We said we hoped so.

"Never saw a show in my life," he said. "Once my wife took me, but I walked out in twenty minutes, and you couldn't get me near another. Whole thing's a waste of time if you ask me."

Gradually, however, we adjusted ourselves to our troopship, and it to us. The men began to accept us as one of themselves, and Flush had become an object of daily comment.

"What is it, an upholstered mouse?" asked one, luckily not in Brenda's hearing.

Afternoons at three Betty Brewer, Elaine Perry and Roger

Stearns would go out on decontamination deck, not for any personal necessity but to sing and play for the men. Brian would introduce them, and Kit always appeared to say hello. The wind would blow most of the words out of the singers' mouths, and the mike would sway so that the girls had to be nimble indeed to keep up with it. But the men didn't mind. Sitting on guns and life-rafts, crammed together in the small deck space below, they cheered them on. Elaine marveled at their applause for what she felt was not really her best effort.

"I know," said Betty Brewer practically. "But at least it's a change for them from that loud-speaker."

Sick bay was just off our isolation ward, and it was there that Emily Lawrence began to show the first signs of what was to develop into a signal contribution, the ability to be of service to wounded and homesick men. There were no wounded in our hospital, but there were seamen who had been hurt, and every day Emily went to chat with them and try to cheer them up.

Gert Macy also found an interest, and spent hours with her face pressed against the window of the operating room, the how and why of surgery attracting her as a magnet a needle. But the operations performed on our troopship were mainly the removal from the impulsive breasts of newly-married seamen of names which did not coincide with those of their brides. It looked like a mighty unpleasant proceeding, Gert reported, so, while "Don't put it in writing" is good advice, "Don't put it in tattooing" is better.

Guthrie and McKay and the others went here and there, talking to the men, and Guthrie told us of one he had sat with in the wardroom. He didn't talk very much, this boy, but every now and then he took a folder from his pocket and studied it. It was long and narrow and spread to quite a width. Guthrie wondered what it was; it might have been some special kind of map, it might have been some new and intricate regulations form. It wasn't. It was something the boy had made himself, a sort of miniature panorama of a house. Pictures taken from every possible angle, put together with Scotch tape so that one could begin at the back of the house, and follow it all around the front, to the back again. Pictures of a small house in a small town, his own.

Brenda was studying Italian; she had acquired one of two returning Italian generals who had been prisoners of war, and, chaperoned by Flush and the wardroom, was learning a few imperative phrases. Bob and I had discovered a neutral corner where we could exchange a word or two, and Betty Brewer had found Lieutenant Robert Hester. She had seen him on the first night out, and had never again looked even sideways with her large, long-lashed eyes. Brian thought her choice good but perhaps hasty.

"With six thousand men on board," he said, "you'd think she might have shopped around a bit."

But we of the isolation ward thought she was doing all right, and beamed at her like a lot of benevolent cupids.

The four strangers in the I.W. were still just that. We tried to badger them into confiding in us, but they refused to divulge why they were wearing civilian clothes, or in what capacity they were traveling. I suggested to them that they were spies, going over to gouge secrets from the enemy, but got no response.

They were more communicative when we were well enough into our journey to also be well into a mass-speculation as to our landing place. Everybody said they knew, and everybody whispered a different name, from South America to Murmansk. But our four Mata Haris were definite. We would land at Algiers. "Or why would we have fifty Negro WACS from Martinique on board, WACS who spoke French and were joining De Gaulle?" they asked.

Actually, we had faith in none of the rumors, yet each new one was seriously and concernedly discussed. This was a condition that was to be a constant part of our trip, and the amazing thing was that it found us always half-believing.

But in the evenings we would go to the wardroom, and sometimes Dennis Connelly would sing. He was the boy who had sung us out of tension that day on the train. All the other airmen would gather and join in, and we would listen and look over to where Betty and her lieutenant were sitting with six people on the arms of their chairs, and four on the backs, and somehow seemed to be alone. And the young voices at the piano would rise and for an hour we would be lulled and forget about scuttlebutt and rumors of subs and destinations.

And then I would meet the colonel and be plunged, like Dick Tracy, into fresh peril.

"Everything all right today, sir?" I would ask, and wait for his morbid answer.

"Well, I wish I could tell you what I know, but I don't dare, of course. Look," pointing upwards. "The radar's stopped. Spotted something, or maybe it's just busted. Wonderful thing, radar. Can't tell you what it does, of course, but it tells you just about everything. It'll even show you an island a hundred miles away."

He invited Bob to the bridge.

"Care to come up for gun practice? Can't ask the ladies, because sometimes, in following the target, the gunner loses his head and swings the thing too far around and before you know it, you're ducking for your life."

The days slipped away from us and the world we had left receded with them. What we were approaching was nebulous, and the ship, now, was our only known quantity. We were in another period of suspension, and it was like being back in Beekman Place, waiting for the telephone to ring. At night the mess hall was cleared for us by Dodie, the charming and indefatigable head steward, and we rehearsed till the ever-present loud-speaker would announce: "All officers, men and civilians to your quarters." We hoped that at least once it might add "and actors" . . . but the Voice, as we called it, disdained any such distinctions.

It never softened toward us, but the colonel took to visiting us as he went on the afternoon rounds of the ship, and with the setting sun he would grow wistful and self-explanatory. "I'm very human about things," he said in one lovely red-skied hour. "I'll never forget the time I took my wife's dog and had it done away with. Never said a word to her, of course, just took it out and gave the vet the order. The dog gave me quite a look when I left it, but it was sick, and the thing had to be done. Then I just went home and said it was dead."

He sighed. "It was the humane thing to do. I like being humane. Fact is, you've got to be these days."

Then something caught his attention.

"Hey, you men down there, stop leaning on the rail or I'll have you battened down in the hold!" he ended endearingly.

But another sunset brought us another sort of story when Gert and I were hailed by a cheerful, robust young man who looked so like Edmond O'Brien of the movies that I never again thought of him as anything but Eddie.

He waved to us from an upper deck and indicated the boy with him.

"Could I interest you in a genius?" he called down to us.

"You could," said Gert.

Eddie beamed, and illicitly the two of them came to join us.

"What did I tell you?" he said to the other boy, when they reached us. "Now, just you leave everything to me."

"Ladies," he said to us, "this is Greely."

Greely was long and lean and bashful. He wore large glasses and when he stepped awkwardly forward I was sure that if there had been a rug on the deck he would have tripped on it.

"Greely is a genius," said Eddie. "I only found it out last night, and I decided something ought to be done about it. 'I'll be your manager,' I said to him; 'I'll see that you get somewhere in life, just leave everything to me,' I said, didn't I, Greely?"

Greely blushed and nodded.

"Stand up straight, Greely," said Eddie. "I want to see you at your best. This is a very important moment for you. Don't let me down, now."

Greely blushed again and stood so straight that he nearly fell over backwards.

"That's more like it," said Eddie. "Ladies, Greely is an actor. Greely is not only an actor, ladies, but a great actor, aren't you, Greely?"

Greely mumbled something.

"Don't be so modest, Greely," Eddie reproved him. "Of course you're a great actor, you told me so yourself."

We suspected a rib was in process, and now we were sure of it, but we solemnly agreed to sit in judgment while Greely gave us an audition.

"You'll never regret it, ladies," said Eddie. "Greely will now act the part he acted in an amateur production last year. Only one line, but what a line! Just you wait, ladies. He did it for me last night, and I was amazed. Let's see, now, you were a butler, weren't you, Greely?"

Greely swallowed and agreed.

"You'll need a little help, though, won't you, Greely?—I want everything to be just right for you. Maybe I'd better be the other man for you. Now, I'll sit here on this rail, Greely, and use the lifeboat as a table. That all right for you, Greely? Well, come along then, old man, and let's have it . . . no, not *yet*, Greely," he remonstrated as Greely made a sort of lunge forward. "I'm not a genius like you, give me a chance to get into it. Walk back, take a long breath and then come in and speak that line . . . and give it the works, Greely. This is what you've been waiting for, this is your big chance, and remember, Greely, never forget, Greely, this means as much to me as it does to you. Let's go . . . this is *it*, Greely."

Greely took the long breath and almost choked himself. Then he stumbled back and then forward.

"I have a telegram for you, sir," he said weakly.

Eddie shook his head.

"I was afraid of that," he said. "Greely, old man, that's not the way you did it last night. Last night you had fire, and, Greely, last night you had an accent. You were an *English* butler. Now try it again and put that old spark into it. Come on now, Greely. This is *it*."

So Greely tried again, and there was a faint suggestion of an English accent.

"Oi 'ave a telegram for you, sir."

"Marvelous, Greely." Eddie applauded. "That was the real thing! What did I tell you, ladies, is he a genius or isn't he? But wait . . . that's only the beginning. Greely can say that line in any accent. Say it in Scotch, Greely."

Greely made signs of demurral.

"*Greely*," pleaded Eddie. "You're not going to let me down now? When I've got you this far? Say it in Scotch, Greely!"

So, to the refrain of "This is it, Greely," we had the line in Scotch dialect, in Irish, in French, and something that Eddie insisted was Russian. We were weak from laughing as Eddie encouraged Greely with a serious face and affectionate, dancing eyes. Even Greely relaxed a little and achieved an embryonic poise.

"Well, ladies, will you sign him up?" Eddie asked us when Greely ran out of accents.

We said we would.

And we wished we could have. We would have liked to have Eddie and Greely permanently with us. And in a way, we had. Certainly they became part of our tour, because they had given us something more than a half-hour's fun that evening on the ship, they had given us a permanent slogan so that from then on, whenever a situation warranted it, we would chant in chorus, "This is it, Greely!"

I think I used it for the first time when small pinpricks appeared on the horizon, which, as we steamed up them, became a hundred and twenty ships. We were in convoy. "I suppose you think that's good!" said the colonel, sniffing. "That just means the subs have spotted us. They missed us the last time, but they're too smart to let us get away with it this time. Keep close to your lifebelts." He looked closely at mine. "Don't like the kind you've got on," he said briskly. "Seen too many go down in them. Oh, give the ship's news back to me when you've finished it; the captain hasn't read it. He was up all night, never slept a wink." I didn't care particularly whether the captain had slept or not, but I wondered if I was going to be able to sleep much myself after that, especially if my lifebelt wasn't all I had thought it to be. I guess I'll just make for a raft and cling to it, I decided. Unless the colonel cuts my hands off. I don't suppose any of us actually ever believed in that hand-slashing business, and sometimes we wondered if the colonel did, but that night as we put fresh water in our canteens, packed our musette bags and checked to see if we had chocolate bars—a nightly routine we referred to as In Case Of—that night I threw in a bottle of brandy. "In Case Of I draw the colonel on the raft," I explained. But I needn't have worried, nothing happened, and the only excitement was when a destroyer drew alongside us. We slowed and a rope was thrown to us, and as we watched, a little black bag was hurried across it. Scuttlebutt soared to the heights. It was a secret message . . . orders to turn back . . . we were going to South America . . . we were landing at Casablanca. "Whatever it is," I said gloomily, "we'll never know." But we found out.

Someone on the destroyer was sick. Our laboratory was fully equipped, theirs was not, and all the black bag had contained was a rather personal little specimen, with a request for analysis.

I think we felt cheated. Nothing had happened and nothing was going to happen, nothing but waiting. And then the next day, we left our convoy, some planes flew over us, and at night as we lay in our berths we slid through the Strait of Gibraltar. I felt unbearably excited at the thought of it, and longed to be allowed on deck to sniff the land and see the lights from the African coast where they had no blackout. Soon we were steaming by the Atlas Mountains. At first the sight of land had been as Conrad described it: "The coast of Africa arose like a gray and desolate delusion." But the mountains were barbaric, strange and secretive. We knew now that we were nearing the end of our journey, and with the knowledge came a tightening of nerves. The telephone had rung.

We passed the islands Ustica and Stromboli, and as the sun set we were racing from one side of the ship to the other. "There's Capri." "There's Sorrento." We were arriving.

Into the perfect splendor of the Bay of Naples we came. Our ship carefully made her way between tankers, LSTs and Liberty ships, all of which had been carrying men to the newly made invasion of the south of France. Vesuvius had the sunset back of her, fittingly gory. We passed a sunken vessel and all you could see was its black nose projecting from the water and there were more and more like her around her.

This was Italy, where our men had gone in at Anzio and Naples and Salerno, and now were fighting for Leghorn. The buildings on shore clarified. "See Naples and die," said a young airman beside me as he leaned out to look. The business of leaving began. We packed, we tried to eat, but the lump of excitement in our throats wouldn't let us swallow. At nine that night we had our equipment on, ready to get off. The dark had fallen fast and we heard Italian voices as a rope was tied to the pier; the barrage balloons were ghostly moons floating around another planet, large flood-lights from our ship partially lit the huge docks, and the loud-speaker was assembling the units for the tremendous job of debarkation. The gangplanks went down, and we were in touch with the land.

Men were attaching a cornucopia of steel to the rope that tied us to the pier.

"To keep the rats from coming on," said a voice at my elbow. The colonel had come to say farewell.

"Well, I hope you get through this all right," he said, with no conviction at all. "I'll say good-bye now; I'm first off the ship, you know. You won't like it here," he added. "It's a dump. You can buy the whole place with a pack of cigarettes."

He strode away and as we watched him go ashore, we noticed that he carried not a package, but a whole carton of cigarettes.

The loud-speaker was calling the unit numbers.

"I.B.67-7432 to the forward gangway. Two hundred seventy-six X-315 to the aft gangway."

Betty was listening, not only for our number but for Bob Hester's . . . she had said good-bye to him once, but there was always hope for another word before they separated.

Guthrie came dashing up to say that a Special Messenger had come aboard with a message for us, but had forgotten what it was.

"But he can't do that," said Brian.

"But he did," said Guthrie.

It didn't seem important, though, for now the men were going ashore, and we hung over the rail watching them, as they poured in a gray stream from the ship to the dock. We wanted to call to them—"Hi, Eddie—Mac—Hi, Dennis—Greely—" but something held us back. The stream flowed on and on, down to the pier where it broke and solidified again as the men formed into companies and stood waiting in the shadows. Silent and aloof, they merged together in the half-light and were still, and we knew why we hadn't called to them. There was no one to call to—these weren't the men we had known on the boat. These weren't the boys who had laughed at Flush and sung with us in the wardroom. These weren't the boys who had danced with Betty on that other dock that was as far away now as the days on the ship that they had thought so long. They had no separate entities any more, they for us, or we for them, they were one and withdrawn from us, they were the Army.

Down the gangplank they came, endlessly, one by one, laden with the burdens of war. They moved in silence. There was no band at this dock, and no welcome but the sound of their own feet carrying them to that irrevocable cohesion.

A ship's officer was standing near us.

"God bring them all back safe," he whispered to himself, but we heard him. We hoped God would.

I turned away from the rail, back to the ship that was no longer ours.

She was very quiet. Her job was done, her errand accomplished. The men were gone, and we felt isolated. All at once we wanted nothing but to leave, too, and get on with our own job. But there was no leaving till our number was called, and the Voice was ignoring us. We felt alien and lonely and we began to take it out in various degrees of irritation. Betty retreated into a nervous misery, still hoping for a word from Bob Hester, but convinced that Captain Bligh and the entire Army and Navy were conspiring to defeat her. I prowled as far as space would permit, wondering about the room that I hoped was waiting for me ashore. Would we women share it again? Or would Bob and I be together, and in either case, would I get a bath? Flush was whimpering, and Brenda was promising him a tree for the morning, a real tree, all to himself. Gert was thinking of telephones, all those telephones that she couldn't get to. She hadn't seen one in twelve days, any more than Flush had seen a tree, and they were about equally impatient.

Brian was restless but not unreasonable about it. Guthrie and I were the worst. Kit was just as eager to get off as any of us, but she was the most sensible about it. She and Nancy settled

down to a sort of game of compiling favorite Martha's Vineyard
meals. It was quiet and composing, but it didn't calm me to listen, it just made me hungry, and I thought of the food I had
left at our last mess, and I thought that even if I had eaten it,
I would still be hungry, as it was now after midnight, and we
had been arriving for about twelve hours. Kit and Nancy progressed to a super-soufflé and I was ready to throw my gas
mask at them, when they were saved by the arrival of Lieutenant
George Keane, who had been detailed to look after us, handle all
the red tape and generally be responsible for us, not too enviable a task at that particular moment of discouragement. But
he greeted us with an eager smile which was brave of him, sour
little group that we were. He was very handsome, and looked
like someone I had seen in a Maurice Evans production, which
wasn't surprising, because that was just where he once had been.
He was charming to us, and soothing, and explained that our
ship hadn't been expected to dock till the next morning, but he
had rooms at a hotel and cars waiting to take us to them, and we
cast off our bad temper and more or less flung ourselves on his
patient neck. With that, the loud-speaker relented and came
through with our number, and like a third act happy ending,
just as we were about to go, announced that Lieutenant Hester
would like to see Miss Brewer in the wardroom.

And so we left the ship and wound up a hill to the Hotel
Parco.

In the dark all I was conscious of was the exciting smell of
land, and I was too sleepy to take in much of our arrival at the
hotel, except that our equipment piled in the hall looked as tired
as we did. But when we got upstairs I became wide awake for
one brief moment. Bob and I had a small room together; it was
plain and neat, and there was a closet in it. I opened the door
and screamed.

"What is it, for God's sake?" said Bob. "The colonel?"

"No," I said blissfully. "It's a coat-hanger!"

CHAPTER THREE

THE NEXT morning we woke early. Now, we thought, we'll be getting at our job. I could hardly wait; I wanted to rehearse, properly on a stage, and I wanted that curtain to go up on the first performance and come down again. Once that was done we would be all right, we would settle down, but until then, we would be on a razor-edge of nerves. But at last it was imminent, we might open the next night. I wanted it to be even that night. If this is it, Greely, I thought, it can't come soon enough.

We were to meet Lieutenant Keane for instructions at ten, but first Bob and I thought we would take a look at Naples.

"Because after we meet George Keane," I said, "we'll probably go right to the theater to rehearse."

So we set out in the sun that was so bright in our eyes that it obliterated the lovely view of the harbor. We walked up a winding street and came face to face with the destruction that last night's dark had concealed; a house torn to ribbons, three gone from the next row, even the buildings that we had seen from the ship last night were only façades, fronts still eerily standing, but emptiness behind. We saw few adults, but thin and dirty children came from everywhere to offer us fresh figs in damp leaves, and, bright and dapper against the ruins, we passed one little man in a white suit touched off by black sunglasses and a shiny black briefcase.

We turned back to the hotel in time to see a miniature comet streak through the door and down the street, with a leash for a tail and Brenda in hot pursuit, and we knew that Flush had seen a tree.

"Well, that's all right," I said. "Now we'll meet George Keane and find out about rehearsals."

We found out. First he told us that we had a new APO number.

"Fine," we said, "and when do we go to the theater?"

"Well, not just yet," he answered. "As a matter of fact, you've got to have a bit of briefing first."

"Oh, no!" we said.

"Oh, yes," he said. "You know the sort of thing, just a few days."

But we wanted to open that night, that day, that minute, and we said so.

"I know," he said sympathetically, "but you've got to go to Caserta first."

So, flat stale and unprofitable, we went to Caserta. On the drive we saw more of the devastation of Naples, buildings gashed and torn, half-standing walls guarding small testimonies of the homes they had once been: a cupboard, a stove, a picture still hanging, or the fluttering remnant of a forgotten dress. The road we followed had been a bloody one. We went down Messer-schmitt Avenue where our men had been strafed daily as they tried to get through with supplies. Now a long line of military traffic passed us endlessly but safely on the other side of the road. We passed a twisted mass of steel that had been the airport, and smelt the hemp as we reached the country, a rotting, unpleasant smell. We passed the palace at Caserta and turned into the army barracks of SOS NATOUSA.

"This is where I came in," I said dourly to myself as we climbed down from the cars and turned towards our quarters, the building that housed the USO players. It was army con-structed, with a central living room, containing a mission table with some three months' old magazines on it, a sofa and some chairs backed against the wall. A wing with three bedrooms opened off each side, each bedroom opening in turn onto a veranda, a pattern that was repeated on the story above. Our room looked neat, and our mosquito bars hung trimly over the beds. They looked placid and innocent, and gave no hint of the struggles I was to have with them, or that they would finally break me of one last civilian habit, reading in bed at night.

There were other USO players billeted there, Virginia Robin-son and Jean Barrère, son of the great flutist, who had been one of the red-headed sons of Father and Mother Day in the pristine years of *Life With Father*. "I like you better with your hair un-dyed," I said loudly to him in greeting, forgetting that it would sound a bit odd to any stranger who might have been around. We fell happily on Tommy Ewell, once of the theater and now a naval lieutenant, who had come out from his ship in the crowded harbor of Naples to welcome us. He gave us all the news we had only been able to guess at on the troopship. We hadn't known about the invasion of the south of France till we had landed. We knew that something was going on, but we hadn't been sure, and we had wondered at the number of ships in the harbor when we arrived. The invasion now accounted for them, all the various craft, and the hospital ships still bringing in the wounded.

Tommy's appearance cheered us up a bit, and we revived fur-ther when we met the corporal who was in charge of our new home, Corporal Bean, whose first name was Valentine, but who was known as Beany of Boston. He was properly pale and stu-dious looking, though he beamed with welcome. He showed us our domain, hoped we would be comfortable and gracefully acknowledged our appreciation of the sign in the toilet which read: TAKE IT EASY—PLUMBING DELICATE.

Beany had a gift for signs and our bulletin board was decked with gems from his pen. DO NOT STICK YOUR HEAD OUT OF THE WINDOW WHEN YOU HEAR THE ACK-ACK. WHAT GOES UP MUST COME DOWN was signed "Corporal B." and also: THAT SMELL YOU DETECT IS NOT WHAT YOU THINK IT IS, IT IS ROTTING HEMP. Every morning, too, he would advance the line on the map a little nearer to Florence, and I would wonder if we would play there, though I also wondered if we would ever play anywhere.

Our briefing began with a talk from Major Parks who assem-bled us in our community living room and gave us a few lines of personal conduct to follow. We were not to complain about the food, we were not to criticize anything. A great deal of money had been spent to bring us over, and our duty was to act and not to tip off the Army how it was to be run; we were never to refer to the soldiers as boys; they were being trained to the responsibilities of men and we were to regard them as such. All of which I agreed with, and I was perfectly willing to agree not to disclose any military secrets, too, but I wasn't so sure about the Major's final instruction. "And primarily," he boomed, "it is your duty to make every man who leaves the theater after seeing *The Barretts of Wimpole Street* better able to turn a knife in the guts of a German."

I must have looked as wan as I felt, because Kit gave me a little nudge. "Take it easy," she whispered, "plumbing delicate!"

But it was not the idea of evisceration that unsettled me; it was that I had innocently believed that we had no function beyond providing an hour or two of entertainment for a few home-sick and lonely men, and so this more bloodthirsty angle came as a slight shock, praiseworthy though it may have been.

"Oh, well . . .," I decided. "So long as it doesn't make them want to turn a knife in us, I suppose we'll be lucky."

But as the days of briefing went on, I began to lose even that small hope. So far, no one except the cast had wholeheartedly believed in taking the Barretts overseas, but now even the cast began to bog down in a morass of well-meant pessimism. We listened to discussions of the play and its probable reception, and there was nothing indefinite or divided about them. Everyone quite simply thought it would be bad. And everyone wanted to be helpful, and everyone gave us lugubrious advice. It would help, they said, to cut out every reference to Italy, as it had been found that when it was mentioned in a film the GIs laughed so long and so rudely that they missed half the picture. It would help, they said, since many of the men had never seen a play before, if we explained to them about the division of acts, otherwise it would be a risky business lowering the curtain. It would help, they said, to tell them that they could leave if they wanted to, but if they cared to come back there would be two more acts. It would help, they said, if we did that after we lowered the curtain on the first act. They didn't say it would help if we never took it up at all, but the implication was clear.

They also thought it would help if we cut down on the love scenes. We were tempting fate by producing a play like the Barretts in any case, but to keep in the love scenes was just asking for trouble. "But they are very real and tender scenes," said Kit. "That makes no difference," we were told. "Give a GI

a love scene and hell breaks loose. Stamping, whistling, cat-calls
. . . you won't be able to go on." And as for the character of
Mr. Barrett . . . if the GIs stayed at all, they would probably
stay only to shoot him. "You don't know the GI," they finished.

We thought we did, but now we weren't sure. And the GI
began to loom in our minds as a strange unknown figure, un-
predictable, uncontrollable and dark. The homesick men of our
imagination were being replaced by creatures from Mars. Every
time we passed a soldier and said "Hi" to him, we thought, yes,
he looks innocent enough now, but wait till he gets in that
theater. Why should he change so, we asked, what alchemy is
going to transform a nice, pleasant, gentle six-footer from Texas
into something that might be dreamed up by Orson Welles? No
one knew why; they only knew that he changed.

Outwardly, we pretended not to believe it, but inwardly we
were all a little terrified. Maybe the Barretts wasn't such a good
choice . . . maybe we shouldn't have come . . . but it was too
late to think of that now. We signed more papers, we attended
more lectures, and we had a visit from Thornton Wilder who
was more excited at seeing us than a playwright usually is at
seeing actors. But now he was a colonel and anyway we were
old friends and we were excited and thrilled to see him. He
brought us reports of the outside world, including the news that
Jock Whitney had been taken prisoner by the Germans, a privilege permitted, he said, to very few middle-aged men.

"You see, they generally keep us so far back that such an adventure is impossible. Jock is enjoying an experience usually
given only to the very young, and the rest of us can only sit
around stuffily and envy him."

We rehearsed, and when we weren't being briefed, baked in
the sun or retreated under our mosquito bars. Before dinner we
indulged in what Guthrie called a NATOUSA cocktail, which was
one of the vilest drinks I ever drank. It was made with warm
Eyetie gin and warm grapefruit juice and it managed to kill any
ray of optimism that might have survived in us. The gin was
not only warm but raw because, as Nancy Hamilton said, it was
easier to age us than the gin.

We bathed in pools. EMs' pools, officers' pools, generals' pools.

We discovered *Stars and Stripes* and the wonderful cartoons of Mauldin, and we found unexpected allies in General Larkin and Colonel Edward Comm who entertained us and were kind and thoughtful and ranged themselves firmly on the side of the Barretts. But they had to admit that a GI audience might be on the hearty side, and in spite of their encouragement we floundered in doubt.

We became a thought fanciful about the things around us, though later we got used to most of them. We got used to the early breakfasts, though Gert said she never thought she would live to see an actress in a collar and tie at eight o'clock in the morning. We got used to sprinkling insecticide over our sheets at night, and retiring in a cloud of powder. But now we each had some one thing that worried us, and the Lister bag from which we got our chlorinated drinking water began to worry me. It was a gray and shapeless mass with a canvas top and a tap that gave up a reluctant trickle when urged, and every time I used it, it nudged at my memory. "You know *me*," it would leer, till at last I remembered a theater maid of mine who used to tell me about a friend of hers who suffered a good deal.

"From what?" I asked. "Ulsters of the stomach, Miss Margalo," she said shyly. And I had brooded about those ulsters and whether they hung neatly in the stomach on neat little coat-hangers or just lay about wrinkled and unpressed. I was never sure, though, exactly what they looked like, but now I knew. They looked like the Lister bag, and the Lister bag looked like them, and for a while I wasn't awfully interested in drinking-water.

Even without this pathological association it didn't attract me. The water tasted of disinfectant and never really quenched your thirst. At rare exquisite moments Guthrie would beckon me aside and ask in a whisper if I would like a sip of American water. He had filled his canteen in the States and had kept it. Then, he would pour me a drop or two, and it tasted of heaven. Other USO units came to join us in our building, and the mornings were filled with the sounds of harmonizing singers, and practicing accordionists, punctuated by the clop-clop-clop of the wooden sandals of the two Italian chambermaids as they went from bedroom to bedroom. Except for rehearsing and waiting there was nothing to do, and we all envied Bill Noon who could at least go to the theater and work on getting our set together and his equipment ready. Happy Bill Noon who didn't have to worry about how the GIs would respond to his efforts, as so far no one had suggested that if they didn't like the scenery they would tear it down. Bill had his own worries however, the main one being how he was to get along with no knowledge of Italian, and a crew that knew no English. The men of Unit 319 were going to help out, of course, but there were three Eyetie stagehands to be coped with. But Bill soon got the hang of it, and it was as simple as a-b-c, he said. All you had to do was put an O on the end of an English word, and there you were, speaking Italian. Marvelous, we said, but didn't believe it till we heard Bill demand el ropo, pronto, nowo—and get it! Bill's progress in languages was inspiring, but it wasn't bringing us any nearer to opening, and we wanted that first performance behind us—whatever was going to happen to us, we wanted to get it done with.

If they were going to tear us apart, then we wanted to get torn and finished, but waiting for it got to be less and less fun. Everyone drew on his own personal resources and convictions for courage, but sometimes it was hard sledding to stand by them. Guthrie smoked pack after pack of cigarettes as he listened to the grim tales of the GI audience. Kit never wavered in her love for the play or her belief in her choice, but she could admit that perhaps the GIs were something to reckon with. The rest of us tried to silence creaking nerves with a padding of pale humor. Brian, who had all the love scenes to play, pretended that McKay Morris would have the worst of it as the villain. Kay, having been assured that the GIs would fill him with lead, was planning on steel waistcoats and other fortifications but Brian told him it would be a waste of effort. "If they can't shoot you, old boy, they'll just get right up on the stage and strangle you."

The only member of Unit 319 who seemed to find the hours rosy and the waiting endurable was our baby, Miss Brewer, but we put that down to the unexpected appearance of Lieutenant Robert Hester, who miraculously had been stationed near Caserta. When he couldn't come to see her, he would fly lightly overhead while Betty dashed to the veranda to wave to his plane as it circled above her yearningly, like the boy who rides his bicycle round and round the house of the little girl he saw in Sunday school.

Actually, we waited only a few days, but it seemed as many weeks before we got word that we would open in the little town of Santa Maria on the twenty-fifth of August.

Immediately Gert plunged off to assemble props and furniture and investigate the theater. The stage was bare and raked, she found, and we would have a tricky time negotiating it, as a rake meant that it slanted upwards from the footlights. It also meant that the floor would be seen from every part of the theater and should be adorned. She dropped in at the palace, and there was exactly the carpet she wanted, fine and rich and floral. She asked if she could buy it, and was told no, but not to worry, it would be liberated for her. Two handsome chairs were liberated as well, and when Gert found she couldn't liberate a wardrobe she wanted, but had to pay for it, she had a distinct sense of frustration.

With the date for opening set, time began to move again. Hours that had stretched to twice their length snapped back to a normal sixty minutes; the camp began to seem homelike, and even the Lister bag looked brighter and less anatomical. Only one thing stayed the same, then and always. Every night, from the first time we heard it, we stopped whatever we were doing and listened to taps. We didn't mean to, exactly, but we couldn't help ourselves. Thin and unutterably sad, it penetrated the dark and melted into the tents of the men around us, and held us bound, helplessly conscious of its implication that went beyond sleep. Off on the roads the sounds of the military traffic mingled with it, and the feel and sense of war closed in on us with the Italian night, and came very near. Perhaps it should have been near to us always, or we should have been more keenly conscious, more continuously aware, but we had been learning more at Caserta than we had realized, and in accepting terms of life that we had not before encountered, we had learned to accept the fact that we were not supposed to be emotionally involved in this business of war, and that it was better for us and for everyone else that we become part of an impersonal whole. We understood it better when we met the men and people of the war, and realized their own unemotional point of view towards their adventures and tragedies, their suffering and loneliness. And we realized, too, that this impersonality was their last defense, their last privacy, and an equal impersonality in us was their one chance of preserving it.

But we had not quite reached that stage of understanding detachment as we listened to taps in Caserta.

Word had gone round that our ordeal was upon us, and last minute well-wishers came our way to remind us again that mentions of Italy were dangerous and love scenes invitations to sudden death. Once more we were begged to cut them down, or cut them out entirely.

But Kit said no. She had talked it over with Brian, and they had decided that they would rather play the play in its entirety, and as they had always played it; and if there were losses to take or trouble to deal with, they would face it as it came, but they wouldn't compromise.

"We may take a beating," said Kit. "But let's not run till we have to."

We agreed absolutely, but then it was comparatively easy for us to be brave about it. We didn't have to play the love scenes. Kit and Brian did.

We were curious about Santa Maria, where we were to play, and this curiosity mixed with our excitement as we went in for our dress rehearsal. I had always imagined Italian towns as colorful and picturesque and vital, but Santa Maria was none of these. Whatever it had been, it was lifeless now. It hadn't been bombed, but it had a drained look. And it was all brown, the people, the houses, the streets, the shabby buildings, as if the Army had absorbed its natural colors, and replaced them with its own. The people seemed to drift in the streets, passing but never touching each other. They never looked at us as we drove by, and we got our first sense of the strange division between civilians and the Army, because, of course, to them we were just another part of the military traffic that pulsed in the artery of their main street.

And then from the monotone outside, we passed in to the red and gold and cream of the Teatro Garibaldi.

CHAPTER FOUR

It was a beautiful little theater, full of proud ghosts of a past elegance. Tiers of boxes rose to the ceiling, the balconies looked down at us as though they still held the echoes of long silent voices, and the oval of the auditorium held out its arms to the stage where the great of its day had walked.

Our set was up and waiting for us, with exactly that look of permanence and security that Guthrie and Kit had been so anxious for. The furniture looked at peace, the carpet spread its roses lazily at the feet of Kit's green sofa, even the wardrobe which had been crudely bought looked as satisfied as if it had been liberated for us with the chairs. Though there were no practical walls to the set, the curtains that suggested them had a substantiality about them, the one door surely led to the many rooms of Edward Moulton-Barrett's house, the window looked on Wimpole Street itself, and Bill Noon's lighting had captured the soft reality of a London twilight.

Feeling a little better, we went back-stage to see our dressing rooms, and found them tiny, which didn't matter, and mirrorless, which did. Apart from the difficulty of making-up without them, we badly needed the reassurance of our own reflections which are, after all, the tools of an actor's trade. Brian made no complaint, because he had found the signature of Enrico Caruso on his dressing room wall, near the spot where a mirror should have hung. It was dated 1901, and Guthrie, whose memory is enviable, told us that that was the year Caruso had left Italy for America.

We dressed, making-up sketchily with the aid of what small mirrors we could collect from our various handbags, and we made notes to remind each other to bring our helmets the next night, as there was nothing to wash in.

As we got ready, the small lift our spirits had got from the set began to sag, and a minor desolation set in. It was not the few inconveniences that depressed us, we had all endured far worse in the vicissitudes of one-night stands at home; it was the feeling that we were awfully alone. Dress rehearsals are never very gay affairs at the best of times, but there is normally the stimulation of those few outsiders that are part and parcel of the working theater. Friends of the cast, friends of one's own, selected members of one's family, odd emissaries from the press department, from the dress designers, just enough to scatter here and there in the darkened theater and make a semblance of an audience, to come back afterwards to administer praise or comfort.

Tonight we knew there would be no one, either before or afterwards, and tonight, more than ever before in our lives, we needed that bolstering contact. Tommy Ewell was coming again from Naples to be with us, but he was only one, and much as he loved us he couldn't spread himself over more than one seat out front, or be in more than one dressing room at a time afterwards. So it was a wistful little company that made its way to the stage to go through the play in a theater that, however charming, was full of nothing but shadows.

The rehearsal passed without incident, except for Flush who picked one of Kit's most important scenes to do something about a flea that had been bothering him for some time. He also decided that he had never seen his tail before and, obviously, the only thing to do was to chase it, a flagrant piece of scene-stealing that Brenda defended as fiercely as any stage mother. "He knew the rehearsal was slow, little artist that he is. He just wanted to get some pace into it." What Guthrie said was another matter entirely.

Slow we certainly were. We were hampered at first by the raked stage which gave us a nautical gait reminiscent of our days at sea. The green brocade of Kit's sofa turned out to conceal a stuffing of concrete resistance, and it was also too short for her comfort. And the slanting stage sent it gliding towards the footlights from time to time, completing the illusion that we were back on the troopship. That tendency was remedied by placing wedges of wood under its down-stage feet, but there was no remedy for our general morale which was going downhill as surely as Kit's Victorian couch. We had waited so long for this rehearsal, and now that it had come it found us spiritless. Perhaps we had waited too long. Perhaps that was it. But I think, though none of us said so then, in our hearts we were peopling that empty theater with the GIs to come, and were at last honestly fearful.

And not entirely because we believed that they would laugh at us, or jeer at us. We none of us minded failing for ourselves. Well, of course we minded, but that would only be a personal defeat. But we minded terribly that we might fail as a unit, as part of the job of war. It was true what Major Parks had said. It had cost a great deal of money to bring us to Santa Maria, and the only justification for it would be if we fulfilled our obligation of entertainment. Otherwise we would be a total loss in money and effort and morale.

Some of this must have been in our minds to slow us down, and also there was always a hesitation when lines or situations came that we had been warned would be dangerous. Instantly imaginary phalanxes of GIs rose to annihilate us, and it made us careful, and a little stately.

When the rehearsal was over, Guthrie tried to take the place of friends and family and even told us that the performance had been very good indeed. But we were all very quiet as we drove back to Caserta, and knew there was now nothing between us and the opening night but a certain amount of time.

I fought my way under my mosquito bar and tried to settle to sleep. The next time I do this, I thought, it will all be over one way or the other. A nasty wave of fright came up into my throat, and I called to Bob in the next bed, but pride intervened and I turned my SOS into a fretful attack on my mosquito bar.

"Beastly unmanageable thing," I said savagely. "And why do they call it a bar anyway . . . it's a net!"

And I went to sleep.

And when I woke up, it was the twenty-fifth of August and the day of our opening.

We drove to the theater that night as numbly as we had driven back from it the night before. When we got there we saw that already a long line of men was waiting for the doors to open, and as we passed it on our way to the stage door, we made a few propitiatory sounds, but we got very little response except from the inevitable Italian children who always hung around soldiers to beg for chewing gum or candy. They grinned at us and called "Hi, Joe," their invariable *ave* to the Army, but as they weren't going to be our audience their friendliness left us just about where we were.

Inside, the stage seemed much smaller than the night before. The two MPs who had been detailed to guard the exits were large and magnificent, and they seemed to take up a good deal of room, and we had an added attraction in the presence of an Italian fireman resolutely pacing up and down in what space was left. He was gorgeous in a bright red coat and a helmet so flashing that under it he seemed to have no face at all. But he was young and amiable and he listened intently when Gert took him aside to explain to him in a mixture of pantomime and Italian that, while the curtain was up, it would be better not to pace at all, but that if he must, then would he please not do so behind the stage window, as he would be seen by the audience. Her Italian was of the Bill Noon variety, but her pantomime was all her own, and we watched as fascinated as the fireman. He bowed gracefully to her, either in understanding or admiration.

"Both, I trust," said Brian, and we left them together and went to our dressing rooms, where we found that Nancy and Gert had somehow procured mirrors for us, or rather, pieces of mirrors, unframed and jagged. Mine looked as though it had been torn from another piece and was angry about it, but at least I could see myself in it, though at the moment that was a mixed blessing.

Everyone has his own special brand of opening night nerves; mine are no worse than anyone else's. They just seem so. Although my part was small, I was as deep now in my own particular hell as though I were going to have to act the whole play all by myself. I tried to shake it off. I tried all my usual makeshifts of self-encouragement.

"Pretend it isn't the opening night," I told myself. "Pretend it's the third week of a summer run in Philadelphia." But that was asking myself to believe too much. "All right, then, pretend it doesn't matter, pretend you don't care. After all, it isn't life or death. Suppose you do fall on your face when you go on, suppose you do forget your lines, suppose the GIs *do* laugh at you? It won't kill you, will it?" But at the moment I thought it would. And I had to have hysterics in the last act, and suppose they decided to have them with me, what would I do then? Don't be silly, I said to myself, from all we've heard they probably won't even *be* there in the last act. Stop acting like an idiot, I said to myself; you're just being selfish, that's what you're being; think of what Brian has to face, think of Kit. Just then Kit's voice called to me, and she opened my door and came in. "Just want to see if you're all right," she said. "I'm going in to see Brian a minute; I don't want him to be nervous about the love scenes."

She stayed to hook me up, and went on from room to room, separating herself from her own nerves to give us each a share of her own strength, which we clung to like a talisman. I felt more selfish than ever, and I didn't want to stay by myself any more. I looked at myself in the mirror and decided that I resembled an old tea-cosy, and that it served me right.

Elaine Perry called fifteen minutes, and I went to the room that Brenda and Betty Brewer shared, though later any dressing room that housed Brenda was known as Flush's room. "He runs right off the stage and straight to his dressing room," Brenda would say, till when we knocked on her door we half expected Flush to say, "Come in." Now, she was already dressed and made up, and looking very precise and starched in her ribboned cap and apron. She was combing Flush very carefully, making a neat center part from head to tail, and telling him what a very fine actor he was and what a hit he was going to make. "Much better than the original Flush, beauty-heart. That spaniel was a dull dog and what was his success anyway but the result of type-casting. Any spaniel can play a spaniel, but it takes real genius for a Yorkshire terrier to do it, and don't you forget it, my treasure." She dashed a little perfume on him and looked up at me. "Hello, Goldenflowers," she said. Brenda lavishes nicknames on you that sound the way valentines look, and ordinarily I adore them but I was still feeling snappish with myself. "Old Tea-cosy, you mean," I said, though I hoped she wouldn't agree with me.

"Nonsense, dear, you never looked less like one," she said.

"That's just nerves. Don't be nervous, Goldie; look at Flush, he's as calm as a spring morn, the pet."

Betty seemed calm, too, and was actually writing a letter. But she didn't go on till the second act, and what better way was there of using the time till then? I didn't have to ask who she was writing to. "He called me today," she said, and I thought love was a marvelous antidote in emergencies.

"Brenda," called Nancy from Kit's room. "Kit says when you've combed Flush will you come and do her curls for her?"

I went on to Brian's room. He was putting on Robert Browning's sideburns. "We'll know a lot after tonight," he said when he saw me in the doorway. "We may find ourselves on the boat going home—those of us who survive, that is. I doubt very much that you'll be with us, old man," he added to McKay Morris who was mopping perspiration in an effort to preserve his make-up and his high peaked collar and stock.

"I've got my bullet-proof waistcoat on," said Kay. "That ought to help."

"Possibly," said Brian. "Anyway, as far as it goes."

I went out on the stage. Beyond the curtain I heard the sound that means that an audience is coming in. But this was different —it was heavier, and denser. Of course, I realized, no women's voices. The MPs had gone to their posts, and seemed to have taken the fireman with them, which was all for the best as I don't think he would have liked the way Guthrie was tossing butts to the floor as he consumed cigarettes in practically a breath. Made up in the character of an aged doctor, he still looked oddly young as he smoked and paced and paced and smoked. I remembered that he had to speak the first line about Italy in the play, and I wondered that he only paced.

From the other side of the curtain the sound grew as the theater filled. Back-stage things were beginning to take on that shape of ordered readiness that means the approach of curtain time. The set was cleared of people, and its furniture had assumed the imperturbability of inanimate things in times of excitement. "We're all ready," they seemed to say. "How about you?"

I looked at the chairs we would sit on, the small things we would handle and touch. Off stage the letters were waiting, the letters we would read in the last act. My own lines hovered in my ears as if already we had reached that point in the night's hour. "Married and gone . . . married and gone . . ." I looked at Kit's sofa implacably waiting, and it seemed to fill the stage.

Then I heard Elaine call, "Places, please, *signors y signoras*," and the murmur of Kit's long gray gown as she came to the stage. Gert was waiting to tell her that the house was packed; boxes meant for six were holding twenty. "Brass or enlisted men?" asked Kit. "Enlisted men; about ten per cent brass," Gert told her. "Good," said Kit, "that's just enough."

She settled on the sofa and Guthrie spread the purple cover over her feet. Nancy adjusted a thin wool scarf over her shoulders and handed her a lace handkerchief. I could only hold her hand, which I did.

Gert went to her stage manager's niche in the wings. "Clear the stage, please," she called.

Kit's hand tightened on mine but her eyes were steady and calm.

"This is it, Greely," she said.

I took my place in the wings with the others who were waiting. No one spoke; we had reached that point where our individual temperaments and nerves were fused in a general responsibility, more intense and deeper than any we had known before.

Gert straightened in her corner and, standing with her feet slightly spread, raised her hand. "*Luminare*," she said . . . and the lights began to dim. As they died the voices in the audience died with them till there was only that immemorial second of complete silence that comes like the holding of a breath. "*Ouverte*," whispered Gert to the Italian stagehand . . . and the curtains parted.

This was it.

My heart was pumping so loudly I thought the others would hear it, but they were all deafened by their own. I think all of us were gathered in the wings, now, waiting for that fateful mention of Italy which we had been warned would start the GIs on the road to mayhem. It came. "Italy's the place for you," said Guthrie, and a thunderbolt of laughter hit the stage. It was true, then, we thought, they would go on laughing and never stop

and the Barretts would go down under a tidal wave of derision.
But we were wrong. Kit and Guthrie were holding the laugh,
just as if they had heard it a hundred times, not showing any
alarm, not even seeming to wait for it, but handling it, controlling
it, ready to take over at the first sign of its getting out of hand.
It rose and fell and before it could rise again, Kit spoke. It
stopped, and the scene went on.

"I dislike milk, but I'll drink it all day long if you'll only rescue me from porter," Kit said on the stage.

"That's us, beauty-heart," said Brenda to Flush, and glided on
like a smart little ship with its sails set. She was greeted strangely.
I had anticipated whistles and wolf-sounds, but instead there
came a snapping of barks and shrill yippings.

"For Brenda?" I mouthed incredulously.

Bob beside me shook his head.

"For Flush," he said.

My turn was coming. I began twitching at my hoopskirts, and
touching my curls to see if they were still in place. "If they must
fall off," I prayed, "don't let it be tonight." I wondered what my
reception would be, and I offered another small prayer, and
promised a better life in return.

"Just so they don't bark at me, too," I begged.

The scene door opened and Guthrie came slowly off.

"Well?" we whispered. "Is it all right?" But the strain had
told on him. He straightened from his croquet-hoop of assumed
age and put a finger to his lips in rebuke. "Ssh," he hissed to his
English-speaking cast. "*Absoluto silencio.*"

My hand was on the door waiting to turn the knob when my
cue came, and I had a last indulgent panic and thought how nice
it would be not to turn it, but just walk right out of the theater
and never come back. Luckily, the hand is quicker than the mind
and I had opened the door and was on the stage before I knew
it, but my entrance brought no comment at all because I found
I was sharing it with the fireman who had left his seclusion and
was strolling back and forth behind the second story window of
50 Wimpole Street. I waited tremblingly for the GIs reaction
to this bit of levitation, but they were either too bewildered or
too surprised to give any, and as I went on with my lines, a con-

vulsive movement in the wings told me that Gert had seen this manifestation, and it disappeared, never to return again. But the entrance of the brothers again stirred the audience to action. As each one bent to kiss Kit, lips were loudly smacked, and here and there came cries of "Pass it around." I began to tremble again, and thought it was lucky that our overseas exigencies had reduced the number of brothers from six to four. If this went on for six of them, I thought . . . but by the fourth kiss they had abandoned this form of participation, and were actually shushing each other. Oh, good, we thought, very, very good . . . that means at least that some of them want to listen. . . .

But then Kay appeared as Edward Moulton-Barrett, the pallor of his make-up and rigid black of his costume heightening the austere severity of his characterization. Usually this entrance is made in a silence which lasts as he crosses the stage to confront his terrified children, but now this pause was filled with audible speculation. "Who does he think he is, a top sergeant?" came heartily from the balcony. "Looks like a company commander to me," came from somewhere else. But again, the shushing was as loud as the wit, and when Kay spoke, they listened . . . and bit by bit they settled more to attention, and when the curtain fell on the first act we knew that one thing was sure, the story was getting them, and when the intermission was over, there they were, in the face of all prophecy, back in their seats and waiting for us.

Then in the second act came Brian's entrance, necessarily flamboyant, his scenes sweeping in breadth to the moment he carries Elizabeth Barrett off her feet and into his arms.

Brian waited back-stage, where each one of us tried to give him straws of comfort to cling to. "It's really all right, Brian. It's going beautifully."

But he was thinking of all he had been told about the love scenes, and our comfort left him unconvinced. We understood and couldn't blame him. The orator who faces heckling has at least the privilege of answering back; he can call for order, he can retreat if it is necessary, he can duck if there is need for it; if he senses trouble beforehand, he can prepare for it, he can even refuse to speak at all. But the actor has no refuge, no privilege of retaliation, and cannot even seem to be aware of his humiliation. He has, of course, the resource of leaving the stage, as a soldier in battle can lay down his arms, but one course is as unthinkable as the other, for much the same reasons. So we couldn't do much more for Brian than tell him not to worry, which was plainly absurd. He looked incredibly handsome in his Robert Browning costume, and we told him so, but it fell on barren ground. He glared down at his exquisitely fitting Victorian tight trousers and beautifully flowing cape. "I'm afraid they'll think Robert Browning was an old pansy," he said.

I told him they had got used to the costumes, but he only shook his head.

"They haven't seen me," he said.

But when they did, it was all right.

He played his first scene as if no shadow of doubt or fear had ever crossed his mind, and he made his exit to a long and hearty round of applause. "There now!" we said, and really breathed for the first time.

And that was the second act—the play was almost over, we were nearly done and it looked as though we were all right. Kit had a light shining in her. With that strange sixth sense of the actor that functions unexplainably in complete independence of lines spoken and emotions projected, she had been aware of the gradual change out front from a dubious indifference to the complete absorption of interest. At first they had hung back, keeping themselves separate from us, a little self-consciously, a little defiantly, and then line by line, scene by scene, she had felt them relax and respond and give themselves up to the play and the story, till at last they were that magic indivisible thing, an audience.

"We must never forget this, never," said Kit. "We've seen an audience born."

When the third act started I slipped out front to stand for a moment behind the boxes in the darkness where I wouldn't be seen. I wanted somehow to be close to this exciting thing that was happening. The theater was so packed the men seemed to hang from the boxes . . . they were leaning forward, intent on the tight-lipped cruelty of Father Barrett. An MP stood near me, and for a moment I thought at least one of the predictions of Caserta was going to be fulfilled, for as he watched, his hand went unconsciously to his gun, and he muttered darkly to no one in particular that somebody ought to kill the son-of-a-bitch.

The play was almost done. The love scenes came and went, and the first kiss brought a slight revival of echoes from the front but not the storm that we had been prepared for. Still, they seemed bad enough to Brian, and when he came off he was obviously shaken by them. "You see—" he said. "You see—" But Kit took him by the shoulders. "Don't you understand?" she said breathlessly. "They're not making fun of us—they don't mean it that way at all—it's just a release—it's just an expression of their own loneliness!"

And so, once understood, those echoed kisses, those cries of "Pass it around," never bothered us again—and after a while, if they hadn't come, I think we would have missed them; they came to be friendly sounds, welcome and a little sad.

The play was done. We lined up for the curtain calls. One by one we walked across the stage till we stood, all of us together, Unit 319.

Unbelievably, the night was over, and we were all, even to McKay Morris, still physically intact. What we were emotionally is harder to describe. We stood before what seemed to be a solid wall of applause. And we were happy and grateful and achingly humble. Gert turned up the house lights and there was nothing but khaki from the floor to the ceiling. Stamping, cheering, whistling khaki—and something like a great wave of affection came surging over to us, and we sent back our hearts in return.

CHAPTER FIVE

THE CURTAIN fell. We kept our line intact for an instant, unable to move, then with one instinct we surrounded Kit. We wanted to congratulate her but we were too stirred to be very coherent.

I wanted to laugh, I wanted to cry, I could only say, "Oh, Kit!" But she was thinking of the men she had played to, the audience she had seen born. "Weren't they wonderful?" she said.

Gert came to Kit and Brian. The Brass was coming back to congratulate them, she said, but the men were lining up outside and the MPs couldn't let them in.

"Oh, but they *must* come in," said Kit. "Tell the MPs they must come in."

The Brass came first, General Larkin and Ed Comm with especially wide smiles. Then came the men.

In its time the stage door of the Teatro Garibaldi must have opened to many glittering people. First night audiences, gleaming in satin and jewels and furs, bright with ambassadorial ribbons and decorations, filling the air with congratulatory babel, trailing the scents of flowers and perfume. But none of them, there or anywhere, could have looked so beautiful or been as welcome as the brown jostle of boys that crowded back to us that night. Brown uniformed, brown faced, widely smiling—incredibly there they were, the people we had longed for, the friends and families we had needed, represented in that line of friendly young faces.

Kit smiled and smiled, and her eyes grew bigger with every handclasp, with every eager word.

I don't remember what we said to them. I remember some of the things they said to us. "It's like a letter from home," said one.

"Have you ever seen a play before?" I know we asked that, and, mostly, they answered no.

"No, ma'am," said one. "I didn't think I'd like it, but you know what? After this, when I get home I'm going to take my wife to the opera."

We didn't know whether he meant that after seeing the Barretts he thought he could stand anything, or whether he meant that we had stimulated him to bigger and better things, but we decided not to press the question.

They stayed perhaps an hour with us, and as the last group left one of them turned to wave, one of those who had seen his first play. "Good-bye now," he called. "I'm going to get me some more of this."

The stage door closed. Like a letter from home, that boy had said. We hoped they knew they had meant the same to us.

Kit watched them go. "They must always come back-stage if they want to," she said to Gert. "Remember to tell the MPs everywhere."

And so, from then on, wherever we played, the men came back to see us after the play.

"I'm glad the lady did that," said one of the MPs. "They've never been let back before. It sure was nice for them." But it was nicer for us.

We went to our dressing rooms, and I began to relax. My circulation was coming back nicely, all but my left hand. Suddenly I realized that I was clutching something soft and humid and dead. "Ah-hh!" I said and dropped it. And then I picked it up. It was a bunch of my corkscrew curls.

"Didn't you know?" said Nancy Hamilton, who had come in to unhook me. "They fell off when you had hysterics; you just grabbed them and hung on."

I hadn't even noticed.

The strain was lifting every second. The theater wasn't a frightening place, it was a darling place. My dressing room was a thing of beauty, and my jagged mirror was a twinkling star. I took off my make-up and years came with it. I didn't feel made of lead any more, and I was no longer holding my breath; I was inhaling and exhaling just like anyone else, and enjoying it.

A message came that we were all invited by a group of Red Cross women for a sandwich at their apartment.

We met on the stage and started out together. We weren't able to do much more than clutch each other in wonder. Then out of the theater we went as briskly as we had faltered into it earlier.

The play had begun at seven so that it was still not very late, but the moon was out and the air was cool and clear after the burning heat of the day. We reached the house. Trees grew around it, and in the moonlight we could see that they had been clipped to make a formal silhouette. Inside, a handsome balustrade led us up three long flights of marble stairs, and at the top a door opened to an apartment surprisingly modern in its furnishings. It was high-ceilinged and the rooms opened onto a balcony which looked down on a courtyard.

"This all belonged to the Germans till three months ago," our hostess told us.

It was wonderful to be where people lived, again. It was wonderful, too, to have some place to go after the opening, to fulfill the need for contact, for talk, that is part of the routine of letting down. It was wonderful to be able to talk normally without always having at the back of our minds the ordeal ahead.

There were sandwiches, the first we had seen for some time, and we were introduced to a creamy substance that came from a punch bowl and was cool and delicious.

"It's heavenly," we said. "It tastes like ice cream and gin. What is it made of?"

"Ice cream and gin," said our hostesses, filling our glasses again. And as we emptied them we talked. We let loose all our elation on our hostesses, and with Red Cross fortitude they encouraged us. They told us we were wonderful, and we told each other the same thing. Guthrie had praise for all of us.

"My entrance would have been better if I hadn't dropped my hat," said Roger Stearns.

"Nonsense," we told him, "they loved your dropping your hat."

"But when I picked it up I dropped my cane, too," he said.

"They *loved* it," we said firmly.

Erik Martin and Chester Stratton had made definite hits. "They loved you," we repeated.

"They didn't love me," said McKay Morris proudly. "They hissed me, God bless them."

Brenda brushed aside her own success in favor of Flush. "My beauty-heart!" she said. "Wasn't he perfect; have you ever seen such poise?"

"I heard he gave the most marvelous double-take when they barked at him," I said.

"He did nothing of the sort," said Brenda hotly. "He wouldn't dream of stepping out of character for anything so crude! He merely raised his eyebrows and they quieted down at once."

The ears of Betty Brewer and Emily Lawrence were still ringing with lupine whistles and other invitations to the dance.

"They loved you," we said once more.

We were too giddy with relief to be more than breathlessly repetitious; we reviewed the various impacts and reactions of the night, and when the time came to leave we even asked the actor's ancient question: "Do you really think they liked us?"

"They loved you," said the Red Cross, being quick to learn.

As we were driven back to Caserta the moon was still high and bright. I doubt if it had often looked down on happier people.

Corporal Bean was waiting up for us. He had been to the play and welcomed us with a mother's pride. "Oh, Beany!" we said and fell into his arms. "Did you really like it?"

We couldn't go to bed. McKay and the younger generation went off for a huddle of their own, and Gert and Nancy, Brian, Bob, and I went with Kit and Guthrie to their room. Brenda joined us a few minutes later.

"I put Flush to sleep," she said. "I want him to be fresh for tomorrow when he reads his notices."

Kit's room was not large but we disposed ourselves on whatever was available. There were the beds, a chair or two, and the dressing table. This was one of those arrangements with small chests of drawers on either side of a longish mirror, with a shelf low enough to sit on, which two of us did. This elegant object had been installed by Beany as a compliment to Miss Cornell. The curtains at her windows were an inspiration from the same source, and had been hung one morning at seven by two enthusi-

astic Italians while Miss Cornell, who had not expected them, was
still in bed. Now they blew softly in the night coolness as we
approached the blissful stage of talking things over in the family.

Kit kicked her shoes off, settled back against the propped pillows on her bed, and accepted her tiredness.

Guthrie took a long breath of his cigarette. He looks most
grim when he is most moved, and now he looked very grim
indeed.

"You looked beautiful, baby," he said. After twenty years of
working together, Kit knows that this is his way of saying that
he has no criticism for her, that he is completely happy and
satisfied.

She gave him a quick little nod of acknowledgement, and asked
her own invariable practical question.

"Was my voice all right? Could you hear me?"

Nancy had been able to be out front and assured Kit that every
word had been clear.

"How did the set look?" asked Kit.

"It was swell," said Gert. "Bill Noon deserves a medal for the
lighting."

"Or an extra cigar," I said. I remembered the fireman. "What
did you do to him?" I asked. "I never saw him again."

"I liberated him," said Gert with reminiscent satisfaction.

There was so much to say, and there was nothing to say. We
relapsed into a retrospective silence. Kit pressed her hair back
from her face and closed her eyes as if she wanted to shut herself in.

Somewhere in a corner of my mind the theater and the stage
and the soldiers revolved in a tiny bright kaleidoscope. I'll never
forget tonight, I thought, never, never, never.

"I'll tell you how I feel," said Brian, as if he had heard me. "No
one could ask any more from life than what we had tonight. It
was a revelation and a privilege." He paused and put a match to
his pipe. "Kitty, my dear," he said, "I take my hat off to you—
you always thought it was the stuff to give them, and you stuck
to it."

Kit opened her eyes.

"Guthrie, too," she said. "We all believed in it, really, until people began to worry us." She smiled. "I'm glad it was all right, though. It would have been a long way to have come if they hadn't liked us."

Her hand moved on the bed and I wondered if she was thinking of her two dachshunds. It seemed odd to see her without them. They always lay close beside her and when she talked she would stroke them or softly pull their lazy ears.

Nancy Hamilton writes with a satirical and deadly pen, but in herself she has an ingenuous bright eagerness. She can't sew a stitch but she always speaks as though she had just looked up, needle poised, from an intricate piece of embroidery.

"I wish you could have been out front, Kit," she said. "I wish you could have seen their faces; they simply lived every minute of it."

"Well, there you are," said Brian. "Why not? It's got all the good old stuff."

We lapsed into a happy silence again. Gert broke it. "I never felt such concentrated hate from an audience as they had for McKay."

Just the same, we said, they had seemed to get more from the play than that. What did Kit think?

Kit sat up and threw out her hands. "I'll tell you this—" she began.

"Yes?" we said.

"I'm starving," she said.

And then we knew we all were. We had talked too much at the party to eat and we had been too nervous at dinner. We needed food now, but we were in camp where nothing can be got after mess hours. Brian put down his pipe and rose in resolution.

"We have our K rations," he said.

"But they are for an emergency," we said.

"This," said Brian magnificently, "this is an emergency."

So we broke out our K rations and triumphantly ate them.

CHAPTER SIX

ORDINARILY, the morning after a successful first night is spent under a drift of newspapers spread open to the dramatic pages, one's usual newspapers and all the others one never sees at any other time. Breakfast is a scrambled affair, interrupted by telephone calls from close friends and complete strangers, and the bath is generally full of flowers for which one has no vases.

We had no flowers or telephone calls in Caserta, but Beany's morning smile did just as well. And for the *Times* and *Tribune* we had the *Stars and Stripes*. Guthrie had been up early and had read it first. Then, since it had to represent his usual after-an-opening foam of morning, afternoon, and evening papers in all editions, he had read and reread it till he could quote it in full, without missing a word, which he did. But we wanted to see for ourselves and we tore it from him. Beautifully the headline sprang out at us: LONG-HAIRED DRAMA MAKES HIT WITH GIS. And the review below it not only endorsed us but presented us with a nickname that was to stay with us to the end of the tour. With the service's love for initials, we had been reduced to our essentials, and *The Barretts of Wimpole Street* had become once and forever the B.O.W.S.

"Just imagine," we said happily, "we got a unanimous press. But Brenda was not so pleased.

"Flush might as well have stayed up with us last night," she said icily. "He wasn't even mentioned."

We had no telephone messages, but we had callers. One of our briefers came to seal us with approval.

"I have fought for a long time," he said, "to give the men the kind of entertainment they had last night. I have written to Washington to insist that what we needed here was serious shows. Now I have been able to prove it to them!"

We said we were terribly glad.

The people who had been the gloomiest in their predictions came to tell us that, of course, all they had wanted to do was warn us of what might have happened, and we were touched to find how many of them had always known we would be a success.

"What did we tell you?" they said, and we hadn't the heart to remind them.

But none of that mattered now; what really mattered was that the EMs would call in to us as they passed our quarters, "You were okay last night."

We were very happy, and then suddenly something came over us. We had been living for weeks in an uneasy concentration, centered only on ourselves. Now we came out of our cocoon and looked up at the sky.

"Why, of course," we said; "we're in Italy!"

And apart from our actor's routine of performances at night, we were free to investigate it. Our daytimes were our own, to fill according to our fancies. We had the clubs, the Red Cross, the officers, and the EMs to choose from if we wanted to go visiting. We chose them all. We could swim in the barracks pools or at the palace, everywhere but the beaches, which were taboo.

"Because of why?" I asked.

"Because of mines," I was answered.

We got our first mail call and retired to gnaw on the results in seclusion, emerging later to share important trifles. New York was still wetly hot. Kit's dogs were enduring her absence. My mother was well. My cat was depressed. We had news clippings that we passed around until they melted. News, even weeks late, was an event. There was nothing in Caserta except the *Stars and Stripes* that was less than three months old, nothing that was printed, that is. Other news came faster. Too swiftly we learned that five of the young airmen who had crossed with us had been shot down, five days after we had watched them go from the ship to the dock.

We wanted to know the place we were in and we walked in the baked streets of Caserta, but like Santa Maria the town was lost in an exhausted drabness; we wanted to see the people but they were the same averted wraiths, avoiding even the contact of meeting eyes. We were to find it the same everywhere we went; we never really saw people, we saw little furtive beings trying to be invisible, trying to keep inviolate the division of the army and the civilians in occupied country.

We went to the palace where we were going to play after we finished in Santa Maria.

We were unprepared for the vast magnificence of this last royal extravagance, set in its gardens copied from Versailles. Even a bombed wing made very little difference to its impressive proportions. It was used by the British as offices, and contained an officers' club and a theater. There had been a chapel, but that had vanished in the bombing. It opened to two miles or so of waterway, and there was also a waterfall, and cypress avenues and small pools and statues. The pools were dried, and the heads of the statues had fallen at their feet so that they looked up at themselves with faint surprise. Beyond the waterfall were more gardens, and the headquarters of General Eaker. There we could swim, in a cool, deep pool which held in its center a small and beautiful Greek temple, which was reached by a bridge. We changed there, feeling that we should have brought togas instead of one-piece bathing suits.

"Magic dear," said Brenda to Flush, "sit there quietly and watch Mother swim the Hellespont."

But Flush had a mind of his own. He watched while Brenda cast herself upon the waters, and made for the further end of the pool. Then we heard a splash and there was Flush, a whisk-broom Leander heading for his love. Brenda, however, had left the pool and was sunning herself at the top of a flight of marble steps. Flush swam on, pulled himself out, tore panting up to Brenda—and fainted. He came to in a minute, and we deluged him with praise and blamed ourselves for not having rescued him at once.

"He didn't need it," said Brenda firmly. "He wasn't exhausted at all; he was merely overwrought. His performances take a lot out of him, you know." She lowered her voice. "And he has never got over not being mentioned in the notice."

To console him, we took him to tea in the palace itself, in an enormous dusty room hung with great gold-framed mirrors and lined with gilt and damask sofas. The damask was tattered but the gold and red still gave an effect of grandeur, completed by the British officers who sat around formally drinking their tea from tin mugs.

Flush revived noticeably and sat up with damp dignity to survey his surroundings. Brenda nodded to him in approval. "Cosy, isn't it?" she said to him.

The barracks were becoming home to us. The umbrella pines took on the familiarity of the trees on Beekman Place and the raisin-eyed waitresses in the mess hall were as cheerfully solicitous as our own Doras and Maries and Evelines. Even the hemp smell seemed no more unfortunate than the passing emanations from the East River barges on their way to the dump.

We were getting to know each other better, too. Most of Unit 319 were old friends and held no surprises, but some of us were unexplored country. We knew that Betty Brewer had sung with Tommy Dorsey's band and had come through without a scratch. We knew she danced as gaily as she sang, we knew she was a sincere and arresting young actress, but we did not know that she could handle a gun as easily as she could a lipstick, and with the same delicate effectiveness. One day, when there was no chance of Bob Hester's plane coming to dip wistful wings in her direction, she went with Colonel Comm and Guthrie for a drive in the country. It was a pleasant day, and the talk might have turned on the beauties of nature and the benefits derived from the contemplation of it. Instead, it turned firmly on guns, and Betty allowed she could use one.

"Well, well, well," said the colonel. "Think of that, now. Want to try mine?"

"Yes," said Betty, who doesn't waste words.

"Well, well, well," said Guthrie. "I wonder if you'd better."

But Ed Comm stopped the car and they went to a field and stacked up three tin cans.

"Think you could hit one out of three?"

"I think so," said Betty.

The colonel smiled and measured off ten paces.

"That too far?" he asked.

Betty measured off twenty-five.

"I'll try it from here," she said.

The colonel and Guthrie exchanged an indulgent male look as Betty took the gun, a sturdy forty-five. Guthrie said it looked very big in her small hand.

"Will you call the shots for me?" she said.

"Why, yes," said Ed Comm, "if you like. Ready?"

Betty nodded.

"Left," said Ed. And bang went a bullet and the left can went to glory.

"Right," he called, and away went that.

"Center." This one she missed. But two out of three at twenty-five paces would have got her a sharp-shooter's medal anywhere where there was fair play, and it was an awed and respectful pair of men that escorted her back to the car.

"Where did you learn?" asked the colonel after a long digestive silence.

"In Arkansas," said Betty. Then she looked up charmingly. "My father taught me," she said. "He was a colonel, too."

It was well-meant tribute, Guthrie thought, but perhaps a little lost on Ed Comm, who though undoubtedly a colonel was, after all, still not thirty-three.

Bob Hester's plane had not come that day, but it came when it could, and sometimes it landed and its pilot came to sit with Miss Brewer in our living room which was hardly more private than the wardroom had been.

"Oh, dear," said Brian, "those poor children! They can't even breathe without all of us hearing them."

But we couldn't help hearing them and we couldn't help being interested. On the boat we had thought it sweet but ephemeral. Now we weren't so sure. But what was to come of it, we wondered. They were both so young, and their world was a tilting one.

"It probably isn't serious, anyway," I said to Bob my husband. "It's just that they're away from home and the setting is romantic."

"Very romantic," said Bob. "The wardroom and our barracks. I wonder they haven't eloped!"

"There's the palace," I said. "I wouldn't trust myself in that cypress grove with anyone."

We played in Santa Maria for four performances, and then moved to the palace. Playing the Palace is an old phrase in theatrical language, dating from the time when the Palace Theatre on Broadway was a vaudevillian's Mecca. Playing the Palace meant you had reached the zenith. It was the ultimate Utopia of the two-a-day. Playing the palace in Caserta had its own cachet. The theater was small and exquisite, a jewel-box in a vault. True, there were no dressing rooms, but the major who managed the theater found corners for us, and while he was at it threw in a good-sized bar where they served drinks and sandwiches to all comers, which greatly increased our back-stage popularity.

Every night Kit and Brian talked to the men who came back, and answered questions about the Barretts.

"And, you know, it's all true," I would hear Kit say. "It's really about real people, and it all happened exactly like the play. Her father never forgave her for running away; he never opened a letter of hers afterwards," she would explain to a spellbound boy. "Oh, she wrote to him again and again, but he never opened one of them!"

"Why, the old—" the boy might start, and then swallow the rest in confusion.

"Yes, wasn't he?" Kit would say with a flowering smile, accepting anything that would make it more real to him. "But in all fairness to him," she would go on, with a quick earnestness, "he really thought he was doing his duty, he didn't think he was cruel, and he always encouraged Elizabeth's poetry."

The boy would go away feeling that Elizabeth Barrett was an old friend and Katharine Cornell a new one.

It was almost time to leave Caserta. We were taking a lot to remember with us. We were going to have to say good-bye to a lot of people we had grown fond of, people we might never see again. Like the paratroopers. Four of them had come back-stage one night, their wide trousers tucked into their high, heavy boots. They didn't join the other men who were talking to us but waited till they had gone. Then one of them went to Gert and Brenda and said that they were stationed at Capua in an old fort, and they had liberated some beer and they wanted to give a little party for all of us, and could we come?

Almost all of us could and did. We went in a truck, a couple of jeeps and a weapons carrier.

Their station was an old fort. We turned into a courtyard filled with rubble and our transportation stopped. We went into a dark building and our flashlights guided us up stone steps to a second floor where we walked down a long stone passage which ended in a hole as jagged as my mirror in Santa Maria. There was still a moon and its light caught the edges and picked out a pile of débris below. The whole end of the building had been blown off.

"Jerry gave this place plenty of attention," said our guides. They led us to a room with one wall gone, a canvas stretched to replace it. It was lit by candles in beer bottles and there were platters of eggs and sandwiches on a wooden bench. We were war-wise enough now to respect cheese sandwiches, but "live" eggs commanded awe.

"And that's not all," said one of our hosts. "We have a little beer, too." They had a hundred and fifty cases.

We met their captain. Captain Johnny Gray of Helena, Montana. Before the war he had worked in a five-and-dime store. At Anzio back of the German lines he had said: "We have two choices, to be taken or to fight it out." They were completely surrounded but to a man they said, "Fight it out," and they did. They held the position for three days and came out of it with sixty-four out of a hundred-and-fifty men.

"You always lose your best," said Johnny Gray. "They won't give up and that's how they go." He was head man of this special service group which had been the first to arrive in Rome and which had held all the bridges till the Fifth Army arrived.

He and his own company had trained in Helena, Montana, he said. He was training new men now.

"How do you pick them?" we asked.

"Well," he said, "I can tell a lot about a man just by looking in his eyes."

His own were the finest and steadiest I have ever seen. He

poured us some beer and asked if we would like to see his equipment. We went to his room which was furnished with an army cot and a table. In a corner his heavy boots stood at attention and on the wall was a crayon drawing of a girl, so young that she might almost have been a child.

He produced his knife, a long thin dagger, and let his fingers follow the blade to its tip. Then he turned his wrist with lightning grace.

"It goes under the heart, you see," he said. "Then you give it a neat twist." He handled it like a surgeon's scalpel.

We thought of the only stabbings we knew, the Shakespearean dagger held high and back of the head to catch the spotlight and plunge in a downward arc to thump harmlessly on the breast of a fellow actor. There was no theater in this clean upward thrust, but there was death.

Bob went back to his first question. "If you're satisfied with a man's eyes, what do you do?"

Johnny Gray was putting his knife carefully away.

"I ask him if he wants to die," he said. "He laughs, and says no, of course. Then I tell him our casualty figures. I tell him our replacements are two hundred per cent." He took out some brass knuckles with a steel blade attached. "I tell him if he lives three months he'll be lucky, and if he lives six he'll be an old man." He adjusted the brass knuckles and gave the gesture of attack, a blow with the knuckles and a down drive with the blade. "Then I tell him I only want someone who can cut a German's throat and laugh while he bleeds to death." He didn't sound melodramatic, and he didn't sound cruel. He looked at us, and there was nothing in his eyes but a dispassionate reality.

He put the things away. We heard a song beginning in the other room. "Let's go back," he said. "I'll get you some more beer."

I looked up at the crayon drawing on the wall and he looked up, too.

"My wife," he said.

We went back to the others.

"*Allouette, gentille Allouette*," came in a fine rich slightly accented voice.

"That's Ranier," said Johnny. "He's French-Canadian. Our company's English, Canadian, and American—only one of its kind."

We sat in a circle singing. The shadows and the candlelight splashed back and forth on our faces. The men were bronze and hard and tough from their training, their faces etched with an intense masculine strength. They were like brothers, we felt, with a trust and affection between them as vital as they were themselves.

We ate the sandwiches and the precious eggs and drank beer and sang.

"Shall we give you our own song?" they asked when the candles had burned lower.

"Oh, yes," we said.

Ranier stood up and looked down at us as we sat together at his feet. He began very quietly, to the tune of "The Battle Hymn of the Republic":

> Is everybody ready?
> Cried the sergeant, looking out.
> Our hero feebly answered yes
> And then they stood him up;
> He jumped into the prop blast,
> He ducked and pulled reserve—
> And he ain't going to jump no more.
>
> Gory, gory, what a hell of a way to die,
> Gory, gory, what a hell of a way to die . . .

They motioned us to sing with them.

> Gory, gory, what a hell of a way to die—
> And he ain't going to jump no more.

"Let's take the empty bottles to Chris's room," said a boy called Phil Huston, and obediently some of us went along. Chris's room had only two walls standing. "My sleeping porch," he explained, as he welcomed us in. The blown-off corner of the room made an enticing gap, and out of it went the empty bottles to crash satisfactorily below.

Ranier's voice still came to us, and Chris took up the song with him.

> He counted loud, he counted long,
> He waited for the shock;
> He felt the wind, he felt the clouds,
> He felt the awful drop;
> He pulled the cord, the chute spilled out,
> It wrapped around his legs—
> And he ain't going to jump no more.

The bottles hurtled, and the chorus soared in crescendo.

> Gory, gory, what a hell of a way to die.

"I'm running out of bottles," said Phil.

"Do you think there's a ladies' room?" Brenda asked me.

"I'll ask," I said. "Is there a ladies', Phil?"

"Yes, dear heart," he said, gesturing largely to the out-of-doors. "Any place on the ground you care to choose."

"I'll come with you," said Gert, and we took our flashes and walked outside. This was how it was when we used to go on picnics, we thought, when we walked discreetly up beaches, or deep into woods, except that now we found nothing more sheltering than rubble. We walked back, and the song met us.

> He thought about the medics
> And he wondered what they'd find,
> He thought about the days he loved
> And the girls he'd played around,
> He thought about the girl he loved,
> The one he left behind—
> And he ain't going to jump no more.

Chris must have got more bottles. A fresh barrage of them came gaily from the gap that made his window.

> Gory, gory, what a hell of a way to die.

The voices were strong and young and the singers looked defiantly alive as they stood hurling bottles like challenges into space. . . . The song climbed into the night—

> The risers tied themselves in knots
> Around his skinny bones,
> The canopy became his shroud
> As they hurtled to the ground;

"That's how they must have looked on the bridges of Rome waiting for our army to arrive," said Brenda.

> There was blood upon the risers,
> There was blood upon the chute,
> There was blood that came a-trickling
> Down the paratrooper's boot.

I saw a fine thin blade in a fine thin hand. I saw a crayon drawing of a fine childlike face, Johnny Gray's wife. I wondered what the waiting was like, for her, and Johnny Gray's voice came back to me. "It goes under the heart, you see." That was about it, I thought.

We went back to the circle. Ranier gave us a great salute of welcome as he rolled out the last lines.

> The ambulance was on the spot,
> The jeeps were running wild;
> The medics jumped and screamed with glee,
> They rolled their sleeves and smiled,
> For it had been a week or more
> Since last a chute had failed—
> And he ain't going to jump no more.
>
> Gory, gory, what a hell of a way to die,
> Gory, gory, what a hell of a way to die,
> Gory, gory, what a hell of a way to die—
> And he ain't going to jump no more.

They shattered the chorus in a final jubilant blast, and they put their arms around us as we all joined in.

Caserta was almost behind us. Bob Hester came for our last performance. There was no room at all back-stage, but they sat together on a pile of canvas that was used to cover our scenery, Bob trim in his uniform, Betty in her delicate blue silk costume.

"I can't bear it," said Brian; "they can't even say good-bye without all of us looking on."

"Maybe it isn't good-bye," said Nancy, hurrying past with Kit's last act bonnet and cloak.

The curtain came down and the Barretts were moving on. The next day we stood in front of our quarters surrounded by our baggage.

"I shall hate to leave this place," said Roger Stearns, as he was to say a good many times later.

We had said all our good-byes. George Keane was waiting to shepherd us into our transportation. We were old hands now at jeeps and recon cars and weapons carriers, and agile as mountain goats we jumped in.

Some of our GI friends were near to wave us off.

"Good-bye, now," they called. "Thanks for coming over."

"Why should they thank *us*," Brian muttered. "We should be down on our knees thanking them!"

We were starting. The dust was just stirring under the assorted wheels of our cars when headlong down the steps of our building came Corporal Bean.

"Good-bye, B.O.W.S.," he called. "I'll be missing you."

"Good-bye, Valentine Bean," we called back. "We'll miss you, too."

We were going on tour, and to our joy it was to be a long one. The long-haired drama had made a hit, and Kit and Brian had promised to stay six months.

CHAPTER SEVEN

OUR FIRST stop was to be at Bagnoli, our theater a motion picture hall attached to the Twenty-first Receiving Hospital. There was no place for us to stay in Bagnoli, but Naples was close, and at four that afternoon we drew up once more at the Hotel Parco.

We were very different from the tired Barretts that had arrived there from the troopship; we were the B.O.W.S., and even Flush shared our new assurance and gave the tree outside the door no more than a perfunctory passing salute. Our first stay had been so short and we had been so distracted that we had taken in very few details. Now we saw that the lobby of the hotel was dotted vaguely with wicker chairs as forlorn as an undusted potted palm but there was a hint of cheer in the small bar that beckoned from a corner, offering a choice of cocktails that included the Dynamite and the Vesuvius.

Our rooms were comfortable, and, for the first time, scattered, which we rather welcomed. We had been living in boarding-school proximity for so long that it was restful to know that if we brushed our teeth or gargled we would inflict the resultant noises on strangers rather than our friends.

Bagnoli was no more than twenty minutes from Naples. On the way there we passed through a long tunnel where the people of Naples had crowded during the bombardments. Outside it we were delighted by road signs that read "Iowa" and "Texas" and "Utah," designating areas under United States Army control. These roads led us to a gateway which opened to the grounds of a world's fair that Mussolini had planned for 1939. I have always been indifferent to world's fairs, perhaps because when I was a child I had found an old colored brochure of the Chicago Fair. It's rococo elegance enchanted me, and I had taken it to school and passed it around casually with the modest remark that it was my mother's summer home. This gave me a prestige in

137th Street that I have never had since and, perhaps in loyalty, all other world's fairs have left me cold. This one, I could see, would have been no exception had I visited it in other circumstances. But now it was transfigured. Beyond the gate and the moldering dilapidation of abandoned pleasure projects stretched tent after tent. The huge ornate exhibit buildings had been converted to hospitals and we passed a stadium packed with medical supplies. This was a fair with a difference, consecrated to a purpose far beyond anything conceived by the Duce, open to visitors that he had never expected.

When we got to the theater there was already a long line of waiting men, on crutches and in wheel-chairs, in the red of the army dressing gowns and the white of bandages and casts.

We felt a new responsibility. Kit was immediately concerned. Would the play be too long for them, she wondered, would it be too tiring on this hot sticky night? At least we could hurry and not keep them waiting while we got ready.

Back-stage we were met by special service officer Lieutenant Hutchins, and we found he had outdone himself to make us feel at home. He had laid burlap all over the stage, provided pitchers and basins for everyone, set up a large container of lemonade and painted our dressing rooms blue. And, in a last frenzy of thoughtfulness, he had placed a program on every dressing table, a program in which he had forgotten to include the name of Brian Aherne.

We heard a gasp from Brian's room, and a few fruity phrases garlanded the air, but when he saw poor Hutchins's unhappy face he accepted the omission with forgiving grace. "After all," he said, "I can have my name on a program any old time. It isn't often I get a blue dressing room."

We dressed quickly; Kit was terribly anxious about the waiting men. "Let's make it go as fast as we can," she said. But if they were tired we never knew. They gave us the same response as the others had, even a little more intensified; they greeted the femininity of Emily and Betty with undaunted whistles and sighs, and they hissed McKay Morris with fervor.

"You can't beat them," he said, when they booed his curtain call.

You can't beat them, we all thought, as we looked out and saw men who had no hands making an automatic gesture of applause.

After the waiting and the long performance we had no thought that they would come back-stage, but they did.

They were quieter than the men at Caserta, but just as eagerly friendly, and they offered their casts for autographs as light-heartedly as if they had been albums.

Kit said nothing on the way back to the hotel, but when we got to the door she said what we all had been thinking:

"I'm glad we're staying here ten days."

We went into the lobby and there, his white uniform gleaming against the abashed wicker, was the young man we used to call "Young Doug," now Lieutenant-Commander Douglas Fairbanks, Jr., U.S.N. He looked wonderfully well, and very like his father, and yet very definitely himself. We bore him to the bar. If ever there was a moment to sample its mysteries, this was it. We talked and listened. He told us all he had seen of D-days in France and Sicily and Africa, which was considerable, and then, like every other homesick man we were to meet, he showed us the pictures he carried of his wife and his two little girls, and we dared a Vesuvius to drink their healths.

What it was made of we never knew, but we had our suspicions. "Lava undoubtedly," said Guthrie. "We will probably erupt later on."

The next afternoon found us on our way to the hospital again, this time for our début as ward entertainers. I was beginning to have new qualms, not for the others, but for myself. Not that I was going to burst into an aria, or oblige with a scarf dance, but all of the Barretts were to appear in an introductory number which Nancy had written for us, and each of us had a short solo. Mine was the shortest, as early in rehearsals Nancy found that it was safer that way.

> If you want to know why
> I said good-bye
> To old N. Y.

That was my whole contribution, but as we approached the hospital it began to assume the importance of a Shakespearean soliloquy. For one thing, I wasn't very good at coming in on the proper beat, and I was also given to picking the key that seemed simplest at the time. But that was my own misfortune, while missing the beat threw everyone else out. So they had evolved a system by which I counted softly to myself and came in when I reached eight regardless of my instinct. Roger Stearns helped with warning stress from the piano, and Elaine and Betty stood by to lead me in with a nod if, in spite of everything, I lost count. It was elaborate, but it almost always worked. "Just remember to *count*," said Nancy, reading my thoughts as we went through the gateway.

We drew up at the first building, and passed from incongruous bas-relief representations of past history to the full dimension of the present. We were taken first to the traction ward, a heat-soaked room lined all its length with men in casts, their arms and legs suspended by myriad cords and wires and pulleys. How can they stand it? I thought, but they were magnificently cheerful. They smiled at us while the mike was being set up and a small piano was wheeled in followed by Roger Stearns who had come out early to play for the ambulatory cases outside. He sat at it again, and we all assembled while Brian introduced us, and then we plunged into the opening song.

I began to count.

"Not yet," whispered Betty, stopping me just in time.

"If you want to know why we're here . . ." sang Nancy.

Betty kept an anxious eye on me.

"If you want to know why we're here . . ." sang Brenda.

Betty gave me a nod. One, two, three . . .

"If you want to know why we're here . . ." sang Elaine.

. . . six, seven, eight.

"*Now*," said Betty and I leaped forward and tripped slightly on the cable attached to the microphone, and missed the beat. I made a weak attempt to catch up, but the others were ahead of me.

We're now prepared to tell you why
And this is why . . .

they sang in firm unison, and proceeded to tell in several verses why they had come over. Why *I* had, I thought, would take a bit more explaining. I retired to a neutral corner and thought of Greely.

"Gillmore," I told myself sadly, "that wasn't it."

The next ward was in a great onyx and chromium building, fantastic as only an exhibition building can be. Inside it, we gasped and thought of Grand Central, except that that exemplary terminal has never been decorated with pictures of Mussolini blown to an abnormal size. Mussolini in Ethiopia, Mussolini addressing his peoples, Mussolini through the ages. We looked again and saw that he had arrested other attention than our own, and had evidently been an irresistible target, for each picture was liberally besprinkled with bullet holes.

A staircase on one side led to a gallery that went all around the hall, and this was the ward. As we looked up we saw that it was lined with beds, pointing to the railing. And facing us, on the floor of the hall, was a room within a room, made of canvas. This, they told us, was the operating room, with four tables where the surgeons worked unceasingly.

Outside it were stretchers in an unbroken chain, with men lying very quiet. Their heads were turned away, as if they were done now with everything but waiting. We stopped. Should we be here, we wondered, would we be anything but an intrusion. But they told us no. The men upstairs were getting well; they would welcome us. But we felt unsure. As we passed on our way to the stairs, I stopped by a boy who looked about twenty. I wanted terribly to say something that might help him, but the words wouldn't come. He must have felt my awkwardness, because he smiled at me. "I'll be okay," he said.

We went up the stairs and heard the faint strumming of a guitar. It grew louder, and we heard singing. "Competition?" murmured Erik Martin, but we hushed him to listen.

> It was in the Volturno Valley,
> I was crossing the river on a run;
> There I got hit in the stomach
> With an eighty-eight millimeter gun.

The player was a red-haired, freckle-faced boy, who balanced
his guitar on his leg cast, and the singers were all men who had
got their wounds from that deadly close-range German gun.

How we were going to do our show in this ward that was not
a ward was a hurdle that I felt was better left to Nancy to clear.
Kit started to make the round of the beds, and I followed her. A
doctor came to meet her and asked if she would like to see the
operating room. I tagged, too, and picked up Bob on the way.
We went down to the hall again, and Kit and Bob went in with
the doctor, but I wasn't sure how I would react so I stayed outside and watched through a window that was made of ultra-
violet glass, which gave the scene inside an unreality that made
it easier.

I had never seen an operating room. I had never seen an operation. I had an idea that there would be both pressure and tension;
the surgeons would work at a terrific speed, the issues of life
and death would be dramatically evident. What I saw seemed to
be leisurely, almost casual.

The four tables were there, the surgeons and nurses working
under the intense light that poured from the canvas roof. X-ray
pictures hung at each table, and the surgeons worked from them
like charts. Sometimes one would go to another, and they would
consult unhurriedly, and to me, watching outside, impersonally.
But Bob, inside, saw and heard more. Their outward casualness
covered a precise certainty that carried the men on and off the
tables with the regularity of an assembly line. Though they
looked leisurely, Bob said, they never stopped for a moment; the
speed I had imagined was there, but no haste. Instead of pressure,
there was patience. I saw a man lying with his leg shredded from
hip to ankle. They'll amputate, I thought. But Bob said they
were remolding the flesh to the bone with the delicacy of lace
menders. The drama I had expected was there, too, he said, in
their sureness and determination to heal. And they were not impersonal. One of them examined an X-ray and chuckled. "Well,
I'll be doggoned." Then he spoke to the unconscious boy before
him.

"You're a lucky kid, do you know it?" he said. "You're going
to walk."

At the theater that night we had a new sense of comradeship with the men who crowded the theater; we had seen something of what they had been through and a good deal of how they had taken it and their response stirred us more than ever. We watched their faces, and marveled.

Kit thought the scenery might have something to do with it. The sight of the compact little Victorian room after the alien spaces of Mr. Mussolini's pleasure domes might give them a momentary sense of security; perhaps they felt that for a time they were back in a world where houses stood in peace and permanence.

"And then," she said, "it takes them into a family, and yet it doesn't evoke their own too strongly. I think it makes them feel warm and comfortable, without any dreadful pangs of homesickness."

That, we agreed, was probably a large part of it. Anyway, they kept coming, and not only to the play, but back-stage afterwards, and sometimes they wandered in during the performance to linger at our dressing-room doors while we made up, or chat politely while we changed our costumes. We were to find that almost everywhere one special friend would attach himself to us, and here it was Blimp. He was named for his general contours, and he was in charge of the hospital bakery. His regular visits were always accompanied by gifts of cakes or jam rolls, and he also expressed an interest in the condition of our scalps. "Dry or oily?" he asked in the tone of a hostess enquiring if we took cream or lemon.

Soon afterwards we found on each of our dressing tables a bottle of shampoo explicitly labeled: "For Miss Cornell. Oily." "For Miss Macy. Dry."

I thanked him for my bottle, marked "Oily," and he told me that for his own scalp he preferred kerosene. I looked at his completely bald head and asked why.

"Best thing in the world for your hair, if you can stand the smell," he said.

Blimp was an Armenian, which may have accounted for that bit of Saroyan dialogue. He spoke Arabic, too, he told us, and when he was in Africa he had often disguised himself as an Arab in order to sell eggs to the Germans. "Of course," he reassured us, "they were always booby-trapped."

We had grown fond of our quarters in the barracks at Caserta, but here in Naples we had a feeling of being on our own. It was pleasant, too, to wake in the mornings unassisted by a bugle.

Kit caught up on some much needed rest and quiet. Betty wrote letters addressed to Lieutenant Robert Hester. Roger, Erik and Chester Stratton discovered the San Carlo Opera, and afterwards Chet brought new zest to "I'll Hang My Hat on a Tree that Grows in Brooklyn," which always brought cheers when he sang it in the wards. The revue group continued its rounds and went visiting as well. I was not much better at this than I was at catching a beat; I never got over a feeling that I might be intruding, and I would hesitate at a bedside till the occupant rescued me with a few kindly words.

Gert Macy said she could approach with a certain amount of ease, but that her conversation lacked flow. Very often it stopped altogether, and she found herself sitting on the end of a bed, just staring. She had only gratitude for the soldier who endured this for a while and then, turning to the next bed, said, "How about a hand at cards, Jim?"

Nancy did better, but Guthrie had an approach all his own. His was not the soothing hand on the fevered brow; instead he rallied the men with a clipped humor that might have seemed unsympathetic, except that it wasn't, and the men roused themselves to respond in kind. It became a little irksome for me, thereafter, when I gathered enough courage to begin a how-do-you-feel-today conversation, to be asked irritably where the man with the mustache was. Guthrie was asked to lecture to the ambulatory patients, which he did, and answered innumerable questions about the theater and its people. "Why was Mae West such a success in 1926?" was cast at him, and his reply was an epic of statement without words.

Brenda had a crispness the men loved, but she called it stiffness. "I come over all British and tweedy, dear," she said. She used to take Flush at first, but she gave it up. "He loves it, darling, but it exhausts him."

Kit always began by asking where they came from, and then,

if she had been there, she would sit and chat about it, which was how she found out about the hurricane that hit the east coast of America that September. She went into a small ward, where a radio was going softly. She sat down with a boy, and found he was from Cape Cod. She said she came, some of the time, from Martha's Vineyard. "You do?" he said and turned the radio up, and Kit listened to a much too vivid description of what was happening right then to her island and probably her house.

She said the men thought it was wonderful. "There go my shutters," she would say—and they all had a fine time.

But our star visitors were McKay Morris and Emily Lawrence. They had a very real vocation for hospital work and a genuine and deep understanding of it. They were untiring and devoted, and we were no less proud than she was when Colonel Cady gave Emily a citation before we left. "We can bill her as the Florence Nightingale of the B.O.W.S.," I said enthusiastically, tossing off a Dynamite in congratulation.

We drank another toast in Naples.

Early on the trip someone had given Guthrie a bottle of champagne which he had saved as jealously as the American water in his canteen. "What for?" we asked. "You'll find out," he would answer mysteriously. We found out when Kit and Guthrie celebrated their twenty-third wedding anniversary. We gathered on the balcony of Kit's room, Gert and Brian, and Nancy and Brenda and McKay and Bob and me. Now Guthrie opened the bottle and filled our glasses, an odd assortment gathered from our various rooms. There was no ice, so the champagne was at room temperature, but it still bubbled.

"Twenty-three years," we said, and drank to them.

"Twenty-three years," said Guthrie. "Twenty-three Beekman Place," which was rare sentiment from Guthrie and meant a combined tribute to Kit and America and the house he lived in.

Where we would go after Naples was indefinite till the following notice appeared on the bulletin board at the theater:

BULLETIN

"Starting Thursday the Barretts are really going to war. Let's face it, it's not a good set-up. The hotel is

third rate and the only one in town. The tail end has
been bombed off but it is safe to live in and fairly clean.
Without sounding like a bad war play, don't walk the
streets alone at night. We will find lots of Italians there
who resent Americans for the destruction of their city.
It is absolutely imperative for your safety to use your
mosquito bars. Don't get nervous in the service. LT.
GEORGE KEANE."

"What is this lovely place?" we asked, and found it written
below. We heard a soft explosion of breath behind us. Betty was
staring incredulously at the board.

"Foggia?" she said. "But that's where Bob Hester is!"

Well, we thought, at least one of us is going to find Foggia
beautiful. And also, we could all stop worrying about the ad-
vancement of Betty's romance. Fate and the USO seemed to
have it well in hand.

Betty glowed, but Kit and I were less happy. Foggia did not
daunt us so much as getting there, because now we were going
to have to fly. Kit had never flown, and wasn't sure that she
would like it. I had, and knew that I wouldn't. Gert went into
conference with George Keane and came out of it with the word
that we could motor but it would be a two-day trip over
bombed-out roads. The flight would be an hour and a half. "Of
course we will fly," said Kit, looking a bit like Joan of Arc.

"But it's nothing," said Brian, who is an experienced pilot
in his own right. "Kitty, my dear, it's like this." He put his hands
together and spread them like wings in illustration of a plane.
"You taxi gently down the runway, and before you know it,
very quietly, ver-ry easily the earth fades away from you, and
there you are, riding in the clouds." He made a cloud-riding gesture with his hands. "I promise you, you won't even know you
are off the ground."

Kit sighed and smiled at the same time, which is a specialty of
her own in moments of doubt. "It sounds wonderful," she said.
Brian told her it wouldn't even be that. "There won't be any
sensation at all," he said. "Matter of fact, it's rather dull."

Our last night came, and Kit and Brian stayed a long time on the stage afterwards to say good-bye, and Guthrie added to his collection of telephone numbers to call when he got back to New York, though he had given up asking for messages. They were always the same. "Tell them I'm okay."

Blimp came with a handsome cake on which he had traced all our names, and then, with nothing in his heart but a desire to contribute to our welfare, he courteously presented each of the women with a box of Kotex. We knew how difficult it was to get. Values change overseas, and the greatest kindness is to supply a need. Blimp's gift sprang from a loving-kindness that transcended self-consciousness, and we accepted it as simply as it was given.

CHAPTER EIGHT

WHEN we left for the airport the weather augured well for Kit's first flight. "It will be as smooth and steady," we told her, "as if you were sitting at home on your own dining table," an odd bit of simile that Kit accepted as gravely as if she sat on dining tables every day of her life. Flush was flying for the first time, too, and Brenda was growing lyrical over the treat in store for him. "Treasure will sail the blue sky in a silver ship," she said, with vague memories of prewar airline advertisements.

But when we got to the field, the silver ship turned out to be a battle-worn B-17, a riddled and raddled old war horse with a record of having once flown back from Germany to England with her tail shot off. The Germans thought they had shot her down, so her real name had to be concealed, but after one look at her, we thought *The Second Mrs. Tanqueray* would do as well.

Gert went to explain to the pilot that this was Miss Cornell's first trip, and Flush made a few experimental gestures in the direction of Mrs. T.'s now restored tail.

"Go right ahead, beauty-heart," said Brenda. "It will bring us luck."

It was time to go. Brian ushered Kit to the seat beside the pilot, still talking soothingly of the easy beauty of the take-off: "Just an imperceptible rise," he was saying as we disposed ourselves in the bucket seats, and Bob disappeared to the nose, where he could take pictures as we flew.

Mrs. T. began a matronly rumble and we started down the runway, a little faster than I remembered from my slight experience of commercial flying. But, I thought, Army flying is bound to be different. It was very different. Our pilot was a happy-go-lucky young man who had never heard of Brian's imperceptible rise. He took Mrs. T. at a lolloping canter down the runway, swerved sharply to avoid a quiet group of grounded Spitfires that he hadn't noticed till it was almost too late, decided there was no sense in waiting any longer, and went straight up in the air.

After we got our breath back, Roger Stearns looked down for a last glimpse of Naples. "My, I'm sorry to leave this place," he said. I was, too, but not for the same reason. Mrs. T. was snorting a bit too loudly for my fancy, and Brian, I thought, looked shaken.

I read all the signs that said, "Break this in case of—" "Pull this in case of—" and shut my eyes. I would open my eyes, I decided, when we got to Foggia or the hereafter, but a sudden bank changed my mind, and I opened them to find that Mrs. T. was flying at an incredible angle, and we were looking down the astonished long brown throat of Vesuvius. Evidently the pilot had figured that if this was Kit's first flight she wasn't going to miss anything if he could help it, and he held the plane almost motionless so that she could have a real good view.

"What are we waiting for?" I asked.

"For it to say 'ah'—" said Erik Martin.

When the pilot felt that Kit had seen everything, we righted and moved on. We had practically been in the crater itself, and I could almost hear Vesuvius cough to get rid of us. I couldn't see Kit's face, but I knew what she was doing. She was smiling and sighing at the same time. She probably did it again when two little dots appeared, cavorting in the distance. Germans, I thought, prepared now for anything, but a glance at Betty's face told me she had a better idea. The dots drew nearer, and showed themselves as fighter-planes in a holiday mood. Lieutenant Hester and friend had come to pay their respects in a series of graceful loops and dives around us that set Betty dancing, and had the rest of us cowering in pure fright. Love could go too far, we felt, and even our care-free pilot got a bit fed up and radioed them to for Pete's sake lay off.

This, after a last swooping curtsy, they did, and vanished again to wait for us at Foggia, which we almost didn't make because our pilot went right over it, and was recalled by Brian who happened to look down and ask what it was. The pilot looked down, too.

"Gee!" he said. "That's where we're going." He pulled Mrs. T. around with the suddenness of a taxi stopping for an unexpected light, and we plummeted to Foggia with the feeling that our brakes were screeching.

Foggia may be all George said it was, I thought as I got out, but at least the ground is solid. Kit came last, smiling to the end. Only in her good-bye to the pilot did she show any indication that she had not been as unperturbed as she appeared.

"Thank you," she said. "It was wonderful—and so *terribly* interesting when we flew right over the equator."

George Keane had not misled us about the hotel. Black, dusty mosquito net hung at the entrance, with the foreboding of a funeral veil. Kit's room looked like a rough draft of a drawing by Charles Addams or Georgie Price, and her window faced the remains of a building that had preferred to drip down rather than fall, and every now and then a heavy fragment would thud to the ground.

There was a curious odor that came from the bombed ruin that was the corner of the street. "Hemp?" we wondered. But there was an exhumation a few days later and we learned it was not hemp.

It was hard to believe that Foggia had once been the wheat center of Italy. Now it was a pitiful blasted ruin, existing only in its importance as an air base.

Planes hummed over it all day long, and at five each morning we woke to hear them as they started on the mission of the day, company joining company as they swept over us to the target somewhere beyond the Adriatic.

Bombed though the town had been, the theater was still standing, and we played in it for six nights. This was a different audience again, for the fliers were like the paratroopers, a group apart with an independence and a spirit all their own. They lived differently, for one thing, with none of the regimentation of the infantry; they went out on their missions, and if they were lucky, came back to their own quarters. They showed their difference in their easy informality and the unorthodox touches in their dress, though in a way these were as uniform as anything General Issue had ever conceived.

Their hats were bent and beaten into a rakish shapelessness that they called "raunchie" and they wore "hot pilot" scarfs, pieces of parachute silk, torn off and unhemmed. They had their own humor and their own pity, as we learned when we heard them being interrogated, after a mission, in a damp, muddy underground room furnished with three-cornered steel stools which were the tail guards that protect the bombs before they are loaded on a ship. We heard the usual questions as to the height of flight, how many planes met, how many in trouble, how much flak. One tail gunner said there was plenty but inaccurate, and his pilot asked him sharply what he meant by inaccurate. "Well," he said, "it didn't hit me."

It had been a good day and all the ships had come home. "Did you drop all your bombs?" was the last question. "Yes," said a pilot simply. "We pasted the hell out of the poor devils."

We loved them as men and we loved them as audiences. They were sensitive and quick to catch subtleties, and they came backstage with a casual assurance; finding Katharine Cornell in Foggia seemed as natural to them as finding her at the Empire Theatre in New York.

"Why not?" said Brian when I spoke of it. "They don't think of distance in your terms; America is only a matters of hours away for them."

I wondered if the thought of those few hours ever tempted them to turn in the direction of home, when their missions took them low over the oil-fields of Ploesti, just to see how things were. I thought of the question that every soldier asked us: "How are things at home?" At first we used to answer literally, and tell them about how hot it was when we left, and what people were doing, and any news we had. But we found that wasn't what the question meant. It meant "Have they forgotten us?" And we would try to reassure them.

Kit thought that was one reason they were so eager to come back-stage to see us. We were a sort of bridge for them to what they had left.

There were only two dressing rooms in our theater, so visitors had to wait till after the performance when we could see them on the stage. All but one. When he wasn't flying, Lieutenant Hester came to see Betty, which was about all it amounted to. Private conversation was as difficult as ever. We wished we could efface ourselves, but if the show was to go on we more or less had to be there, chaperons in spite of ourselves. But they seemed content, standing together in the wings.

Brian shook his head over them. "The trouble is," he said, "they'll get so used to having us around they'll be scared to death if they ever find themselves alone."

We wondered again how serious it was, but Betty kept her counsel. However, we noticed that she had very little interest in joining us on parties, and practically none when she did, and I found her once in a corner indulging in a game of solitaire and leaving a fine assortment of generals, colonels, and majors to make out as best they could with Gert and myself.

The hospital had asked us to go out and do the revue and a message came to Brian from the head of the Red Cross there. "Good Heavens!" he said when he came to the signature. "It's Madeleine Carroll!"

She met us when we went out, lovely as ever. We knew the marvelous work she had done, and that she had given everything up for it, but it wasn't until we saw her, uniformed and on duty, that we really knew all it meant to her.

It meant something to the men, too. She had sincerely tried to work under her married name of Hamilton, but the men knew Madeleine Carroll when they saw her and that was how they wanted her, though the hospital supplies took a slight beating as a result. Toothbrushes and soap went like snowflakes till a check was made and it was found that anything given out by Miss Carroll was preserved as a souvenir, or if they could get her to autograph it, sent home as a trophy.

She showed us the hospital, well planned to give as much privacy as possible. The patients were mostly fliers, though not all of them had suffered in the line of duty. Three who were badly hurt had got their injuries sleep walking, and Emily couldn't help feeling slightly thwarted when she discovered that she had spent hours cheering up a patient who was suffering from nothing more serious than hemorrhoids.

But the seriousness was there, though the men tried to cover it with that never-changing, "I'm okay," and sometimes it was too insistent for even their courage.

We were waiting in a corridor, on our way to a ward, when a doctor came out of an isolated room. He stopped and spoke to two fliers who were just going in. Madeleine took me to the open door. "Look," she said, in a very low voice. "This is such a wonderful boy. We're trying to hold on to him with every breath we draw."

I looked in, and saw him in the bed, his mouth and nose covered by an oxygen mask. The two fliers were standing, one on each side of him, their faces set, and they each held one of his hands as if they were trying to give him some of their own strength.

The doctor came back, and they looked at him with a question, but he looked past them, to the boy. "Well, do everything you can, doc," they said, and started to leave. "We'll be seeing you, pal," they said from the door, and they walked away, their steps sounding slowly down the corridor.

I asked Madeleine what had happened to him. "Flak—in the stomach," she said. "There's just a thread of hope, but he's so weak—" She broke off and beckoned to Betty.

"Could you sing something very softly? It might just reach him and help him to turn the corner."

Obediently Betty went in, and stood at the foot of the bed. His eyes were clouded with pain, but all at once they focused. He stared at her, and then he snatched off his mask and smiled and waved, but he waved as though she were a long way off. His face contorted in a struggle for breath, and the doctor put the mask in place again. Betty waited a moment and then in a half-voice she began to sing as truly and steadily as if there were no tears streaming down her face. But the focus was lost, and in the morning he was gone.

CHAPTER NINE

FROM Foggia we went to Bari, again by plane. We hoped that Kit's second trip would be less whimsical, but when we saw the pilot and recognized him as the same we settled into our bucket seats and prepared for the worst, which we got, topped off by a landing when he bounced so high that it was easier for him to keep on going up again. Then, after an uneasy circle or two, he tried again and this time we stayed down. Kit seemed unaware that this was not the usual method, so we thought it best not to enlighten her, but Brian was grim. "It's all very well," he said. "He has come out of these things so far, but luck like that can't last, and I don't want to be with him when it runs out "

It looked as though our own luck was beginning to fray. There may be noisier hotels than the one we were quartered at, but I hope never to know them. There was a water pump that dredged the basement, which needed it. There was a near-by military band that believed, mistakenly, that practice makes perfect. Beside us was a very active night club called the COD, the initials standing for Corporals On Down. This kept us well awake till two each morning, to be roused again at dawn by a conscientious rooster. This last we thought we could do something about, but we found he was a fellow actor, a valued member of a USO variety act, and short of complaining to Equity we were helpless.

We began to look a bit dark-eyed and pale, and only came to life at the theater. Here again we had a totally different audience but the response gave us the same sense of wonder and gratitude.

The uniforms back-stage afterwards told us how varied the audience had been. Poles, Yugoslavs, South Africans, Negroes, Russians, and British, as well as our own men. Yet they came as if the Barretts were old and welcome friends.

All of them had been away from home a long time. We looked at hundreds of snapshots of wives and sisters and sweethearts and families; they would bring them out as if the act of showing them made them more actual. Sometimes they would look at them as if they, too, were seeing these faces for the first time. Then, as we talked about them, familiarity would return, and they would put them back in their wallets with a sort of relief. We were to see so many of these wallets. Sometimes lying on the stretchers of the wounded, sometimes stacked, waiting to be sent home, and in all of them were the small photographs that were the only links with far-away homes.

We found that most of the British who were down from the front line referred to it as the Polish front. We said we didn't know there was one.

"The Poles are holding some of the worst positions up north, so we call it that," they explained.

It was always exciting to talk with them, and we never got used to their wanting to. "You see," Kit said again, "it's the sense of being with a family. They have seen us as one in the play, and they think of us as one."

As a family off-stage we had our first disruption. We had been warned about the GI trots, or dysentery, and here it caught up with us. My Bob was the first victim, and was put in hospital, and we left him there when we went on to Lecce. It was raining too hard for even our pilot to care about flying, so we went by bus. As we passed through the towns, I noticed how many buildings had the Hammer and Sickle painted on them, and I wondered what the Italians had done about those large stencils of Mussolini that used to stare at you from every wall space.

Lecce is a quaint town, full of baroque churches. It was probably very picturesque, but it was also very wet. It rained in Lecce. It rained in the hotel and it rained in the theater, especially on the stage, and particularly on Brian who had to spend a lot of time stage center where the stream was steadiest. Our gloom deepened. Keinert Wolff fought the dysentery for a while but had to go to hospital, and Chester Stratton played his part as well as Bob's, but he couldn't play two brothers at once, so we cut one out. "If this goes on," said Guthrie wearily, "we can call it *The Barrett of Wimpole Street*.

Kit stayed well, but her room at the hotel had implications that depressed her. It had five beds.

"I might as well be in a ward and have done with it," she said.

"Well," we said, "if it gets too bad we'll come and do the revue for you."

My own room was dark and high; I could see the one light that depended from the ceiling if I used my flashlight. At night I retired with a book in one hand, and a candle in the other, feeling a good deal like the last days of Bernadette.

Betty was worrying about Bob Hester and often she brushed at her eyes when she was making up. "It's the mascara," she would explain. "It always makes them water."

I was worrying about my own Bob, though I shed no tears. Instead, I became increasingly cross.

Brenda suggested finally that she thought exercise would do me good. "A nice walk, Goldie," and even offered me Flush as a companion. "Though you may have to carry him," she added. "He hates getting wet." I hated it too but, declining Flush, I went out one afternoon when the rain was less prodigal. The square was gray and medieval, and from the cathedral a procession of priests passed in red and purple robes. I went down one of the twisting streets and stopped to look at an old doorway. "If I were in a better temper," I thought, "I could imagine it might have belonged to the Capulets." Two young soldiers came along and stopped, too. "I declare," said one; "it's an American girl. Give her a poke, buddy, and see if it's true." They grabbed my arm and beamed at me. "What were you doing, honey?" they asked. I said I was just walking.

"Just walking?" The horror in their voices implied that I had met a fate worse than death.

"Well, you're on the town with us, now, U.S.A. But talk," they begged me. "Go on and talk good old American." I asked if they had had a lot of vino. "Hear that voice," they said. "She's surely from the States."

I was entwined by an arm of each. "You're with us from now on," they said, a mass of youth and vitality. I tried to rally a few defunct girlish spirits. "I'd love to be," I said, hoping I would be up to it.

They went into an earnest conference as to what they could do for an American girl.

"I know," said one. "She'd like to see a beautiful estate. Wouldn't you like to see the most beautiful estate in the whole world, darling?"

"You don't know any," said his friend.

"Oh, yes, I do. This is a stinking no-good town, but I do know a beautiful estate here."

"You won't be able to find it," said the doubter. His friend brushed this aside and asked me if I was afraid of walking. I said I'd love to walk to the estate.

"All right," said the other, "but he'll never find it."

We started off, their arms firmly in mine, one telling me how beautiful the place would be, the other insisting that we would never find it. But after considerable walking we got to a handsome house surrounded by a high hedge.

"See, darling? Isn't that beautiful? Wait till you see inside."

"Are we going in?" I asked.

"Of course we're going in," they said. I heard a dog bark. "Never mind him," they said. "We'll just kick him in the teeth." No dog appeared, though, as we started up a gravel path to the house, and no one came to stop us. My friends led me to the back, and a gardener approached.

"Our sister," said my guides, "would like to see the estate."

I hoped the gardener wouldn't understand English, but he did.

"Impossible," he said.

"Impossible? Impossible for our sister?" Their voices were strong and incredulous. "Ask the owner to come down."

I felt stiffly shy now, and said that what I had seen had been lovely, and not to bother.

"You're going to see everything," they said. "Inside and out."

With this decision they stepped up to an imposing door and beat on it. To my relief no one answered. But they raised lungs of iron and shouted, "Paysan—paysan!"

"What's that mean?" I asked, hoping to distract them.

"It means friend," they said. "That's what you got to call them."

With that four people appeared on the veranda above and

looked down at us with understandable surprise. I smiled as placatingly as I could, and hoped I looked more respectable than I felt.

"Our sister would like to go through your house," said my friends.

"No, no," I murmured, but they silenced me.

"Yes, sweetheart, you'll love it. We can show our sister anything she wants to see," they said, giving me what I feared wouldn't impress the people above us as brotherly squeezes.

One of the owners came down to us. "I'll be delighted to show you around the garden," he said, and I managed to stifle my companions' irritation at this compromise. We went around the really lovely, though dripping, garden, and my brothers recovered their enthusiasm. "Isn't this the best place you've ever seen in Italy?" they kept saying.

I thanked our gracious guide and my brothers flung their arms around me and said, "Okay, paysan," and we went away without hostilities.

As we walked back one of them took my hat off. "My goodness," he said, "what lovely hair." He started patting it, and so did the other.

"Our sister has beautiful, lovely American hair," they chanted.

Each held one of my hands tightly and they would stop and gaze at me so earnestly that I almost felt my features were being erased, and I hoped that what was left of my face wouldn't slip to the shiny wet pavement and splinter to pieces before their eyes.

"Our sister has a sweet face, hasn't she?" they said. "And look at that American nose." They looked at it and threw themselves on me in another demonstration of approval. "Now we'll all have dinner together, and we'll take you dancing."

I explained why I couldn't join them. I had to be at the theater, I said.

"Our sister's in a show!" they shouted. "That's wonderful. I'll bet she sings and dances and is the best thing in it. We'll be in the front row cheering, and we'll take you whirling afterwards."

I wanted to tell them that my part was very small and staid, I wanted to tell them that I could more nearly be their mother than their sister, but their enthusiasm seemed more important than my reality, so I let it go.

In the hotel lobby they overwhelmed me in embraces of affectionate farewell, much to the astonishment of Brian, who happened along just then.

"Don't forget," they said. "We showed you the most beautiful estate you've ever seen. Don't forget, promise?"

"No, no," I said, "I promise."

"Who were your friends?" asked Brian when they had gone. I realized I didn't know their names, but it didn't matter. "They were my brothers," I told Brian, and it seemed quite true.

It kept on raining, but there was a slight lift in our spirits. Brenda had got word that Sergeant Frederick Voight had a special leave and would meet her in Rome. Sergeant Voight had been an actor and Brenda had acted with him in the first production of the Barretts, and had also married him. She had thought that they might possibly meet on our trip but had not really dared to hope, but here he was, and she was tiptoe in excitement.

How do you suppose he'll take to Flush? we wondered, though since Flush bit anyone who went near Brenda, it was more important how he would take to the sergeant. "Treasure will understand," said Brenda.

"I hope Fred will," said Gert.

Betty had had news of her Bob, and the mascara was less troublesome, and my Bob and Keinert returned to the fold. Bob had been in a ward with four airmen; one of them had been a Bulgarian prisoner of war, and had told Bob something of the treatment he had endured. The last delicacy, he had said, was to be put with other prisoners of war in cages in the zoo to be exhibited by guides to parties of Bulgars as examples of American gunmen.

It poured the day we left, but we were going to fly notwithstanding. "But not with the same pilot," said Brian firmly; "I'll walk to Rome first."

"I think," said Gert, when we got to the airport, "that you're going to have to walk, Brian," for there, waiting for us, was our old insouciant Icarus.

I'm sure if there had been any other transportation Brian would have taken it and I would have been the first to follow him, but there wasn't. We boarded the plane, shut our eyes and gave up. But we opened them again to stare at each other. The take-off was perfect, and Kit looked startled. "Is anything wrong?" she seemed to say, but everything was fine. We flew steadily and serenely, leaving the rain behind us, to a landing as smooth as velvet.

"Well," said Brian to the pilot. "Jolly good."

"Yes," said the pilot. "I'm feeling better." We asked if he had been ill, which might have accounted for his earlier acrobatics. "I've just had a baby," he said, as if we should have noticed his condition before. We heaped him with congratulations and questions.

"It's a little girl," he told us, and his voice lingered gently on the word. "I heard two days ago; she's ten days old now."

The sun was bright in Rome, and the Grand Hotel welcomed us warmly, and there was a message at the desk for Brenda.

"Sergeant Voight is waiting upstairs for Miss Forbes."

"Someone hold Magic," said Brenda, and tossed Flush to us like a bridal bouquet, and fled.

We had flown low over Cassino on our way to Rome and had seen it lying in the bright sunlight and we were haunted by memories of the terrible struggle that had taken place there. We had come from the crumpled towns of Foggia and Bari, and Rome seemed like another world. The women were smart and well groomed, and the people looked as if they belonged to themselves, just as Rome was still itself. The Army had not absorbed it, its color was the same, it was intact and exciting. The Teatro Eliseo where we played was neat and modern and intensified our feeling of being in a city that had not been engulfed by the destruction around it.

We might have been coming back to New York after a long tour of one-night stands, and I thought so even more when I found that Kit's dressing room and mine bloomed with flowers.

"Read the card," said Gert; "hurry and read it." Clumsily I tore open the envelope. "Major Robert Flemyng." I couldn't believe it. Bobby Flemyng, our darling Bobby who had played with Kit in *No Time For Comedy*. I had played in it, too, and loved Bobby as much as Kit did. He had left us when he first suspected that he might be needed in his native England, and got there the day war was declared. He had been five years in the infantry and had received the MC and we had heard that his hair had turned white, though we couldn't think of him as anything but the gay and deft young actor we had last seen, full of what the Irish call dirty charm.

Gert said he was out front, and I'm afraid we played exclusively for him that night, and waited anxiously for him to come back afterwards. When he came he was just as we had last seen him, not a gray hair and the dirty charm was as evident as ever.

"How did you know we were here?" we asked when we had given him a thorough welcome.

"I didn't," he said, wiping some of our make-up off his face. "I was given a furlough, and as my jeep turned by the Colosseum the headlights hit a poster. I saw Katharine Cornell and Brian Aherne in large letters and I thought I was dreaming. I damn near ran smack into it."

He had been at Dunkirk and Africa, now he was at Rimini in charge of a company of Cyprians. "Poor devils," he said. "They haven't the remotest idea of what it's all about, but they're grand fighters." We asked about his MC which we knew he had got in Africa for taking ammunition cars over mined roads.

"Oh, that was the ham in me," he said. "They asked for volunteers, and to my horror I found myself stepping forward. Just my actor blood, picking up a cue."

We wished he could have stayed with us, but his furlough was short. His five years could have got him a long one at home, but he said he didn't think he'd take it. "Not just yet," he said. "I think I'll wait till I get those poor beggars of mine back to the Isle of Cyprus."

We found the other soldiers who came to see us were on furloughs, too. Rome was a rest town for them, and they loved it, though they were bitter about the rest of Italy, and the lines in the play referring to it were still greeted with yells of derision. There was plenty of amusement for them, the Red Cross had wonderful tours arranged for them, and people gave concerts in their palazzi, and there was another theater, which housed an Italian production of Clare Boothe's play *The Women*. Everything was made very comfortable for the men, and there was a sort of vacation feeling everywhere, which was only natural, and we fell in with it. We lost our sense of being a unit, and went our own ways. We saw paintings and heard music and went sightseeing. We were tremendously comfortable, too, and the hotel had hot water, a luxury that made us curious. Kit heard that it was for the benefit of a Brazilian general who was there, and seeing him with his aide she stopped and asked that he tell the general that we were very grateful for his presence, and to thank him for the hot water. The aide translated this and then replied that the general was just about to offer his own thanks, as he understood he owed the hot water to the presence of Miss Cornell.

We found friends in Rome. Natalia Murray, a Roman born American friend of Kit's and mine, was in the Psychological Warfare Branch, and she came to see us, and to beg Kit to give a performance for civilians. Kit thought about it, and decided that she would do it as a gesture from American actors to the memory of Eleanora Duse. The Army was nice about red tape, and Natalia was a whirlwind of purpose, and before we knew it we found ourselves at ten-thirty one morning going through what was billed for that performance only as *La Famiglia Barrett*.

The audience was charming and polite, but we had grown used to our uninhibited GIs and we missed the whistles and hisses. When the references to Italy went unchallenged we almost forgot our lines, and at times *La Famiglia Barrett* had to watch that it didn't break into giggles when it found itself waiting for reactions that didn't come.

Afterwards we had tea in the lobby of the theater with Prince Doria, then mayor of Rome, as host. "You know he was imprisoned by the Fascists for nine years, don't you?" said Natalia. I said I didn't know. "Oh, yes," she said. "Three of them were in solitary confinement." She pointed out a number of people who had experienced imprisonment, and a man whose wife had gone mad because he had been half an hour late one day and she thought he had been picked up by the Gestapo.

Natalia explained that they had never known when that would happen. "That's why I was so anxious for Kit to give them this matinee," she said. "For so long they had no life of any kind, they didn't dare even to leave their homes, they had nothing but fear and privation." Her sister's husband had been picked up, but luckily his release had been procured in time to save him from being machine-gunned and dynamited with three hundred and twenty others in reprisal for six slain Germans. She told us this as simply as if he had missed a train.

Prince Colonna was there. His wife was an old friend of mine from America; between them they had helped over fifty Americans and British to escape and there were two death sentences on his head. "Of course," he said to me, "one death sentence is ample, but we are a redundant nation."

Looking at these gracious, finely drawn people drinking tea and making pleasant conversation, it was hard to believe that they had suffered and fought tyranny in their own way. Walking back to the hotel with Bob, in the sunlit richness around us already they began to seem faint and legendary. As long as a city stands, I thought, and its people keep an outward show, it's treacherously easy to minimize fact.

Our ten days in Rome went very quickly, and somehow we didn't mind. It was lovely to be comfortable and come and go as we pleased, but I think we all had a little the feeling that that wasn't what we had come over for, and we felt restive.

Being in Rome was like walking on a thick red carpet after a cindery path, but we wouldn't be sorry to pick up the path again. It was going to take us to Florence, where we would play to the Fifth Army and that was thrilling to think of, and we had another excitement to beckon us there.

Betty and Bob Hester were going to be married in Florence if Bob could get a waiver. "He's supposed to wait six months," Betty told us, "but we hope it can be arranged."

They had been engaged ever since Caserta. "I knew that cypress grove wasn't safe," I said as I hugged her. "But why didn't you tell us before?"

She said they had wanted to be sure. "We're so far from home and he wasn't sure he wanted me to stay on the stage and—oh, lots of things." I could imagine what they were. I remembered the hospital at Foggia and the planes that went out and didn't come back.

"But we've settled everything," she said. "Now all we have to do is pray for that waiver." She wiped her eyes.

"Mascara?" I asked.

She nodded and smiled. "It's awful stuff, isn't it?" she said.

With Betty's news we stopped being independent and became a family again. Brenda was to be matron of honor and was frantically trying to assemble a worthy costume. She had a dress she thought would do, but she didn't have a hat. Betty thought it would be perfect if she could get enough parachute silk to make a wedding dress. Gert had taken over the matter of the waiver and was being busy and mysterious, and the rest of us were consulting about wedding presents. "Something they can pack easily," we kept reminding each other. "Of course," said Nancy and went out and bought a whole set of dishes.

From the moment he knew we were to play in Rome, Bill Noon had had one great hope, and just before we left it was realized. Special Service arranged that we would have an audience with the Pope. Not for ourselves alone, of course. The narrow audience chamber was packed with men and women of all branches of the service. Here and there we saw a woman in the high-necked black dress and veil that is as compulsory as the train and three feathers of a presentation at Court, but they were very few and lost in the preponderance of uniforms.

I remember the long wait, and the growing tension, and the warning murmur as the secretaries appeared, gorgeous heralds in purple and crimson. Then there was a movement like a flight of birds. It was the hands of the soldiers stretching up to the figure in white borne above them on a dais. Leaning forward, the Pope touched the hands, as he was taken to the great golden chair at the end of the chamber. He spoke in Polish and French and English, and I thought his gestures were the most beautiful I had ever seen. Then, at the end, he came down amongst us with a word for each. When he came to me he asked if I were an American, and I told him yes. He made the sign of the cross and laid his hand on mine and it was so light I might have dreamt it.

"My blessing to America and all you love there," he said, and moved away.

Impressive to anyone, to our Catholics it was a spiritual experience I could only guess at. I watched as he went to Bill Noon. Bill had been preparing for days, and he was so hung with rosaries to be blessed for his family and friends that he looked a bit like a bead curtain, but his face was serious as I had never seen it. When the Pope reached him, Bill swayed, and I thought he was going to faint, but he steadied and received the blessing. He had told us that this would be the fulfillment of his life, and seeing him, we knew he meant it.

That was the last of Rome. We were to have three days in Sienna, and then Florence and the Fifth Army.

CHAPTER TEN

THE WAY to Florence was a gray-green tapestry of hills and olive trees and little villages as soft and helpless as kittens. The spoor of war was everywhere. Twisted railroad tracks, blasted bridges, German tanks, burnt-out planes, and each mile brought us nearer to combat zone.

It was dusk when we got to the Hotel Excelsior, and very cold, but there were British officers in the lounge and that meant there was tea, and they gave us a warming cup, but before we had finished it all the lights went out, and we retired with candles to our rooms. The rooms had the smell of chalk and erasers common to recently bombed places, which comes from the plaster that continues to fall in a fine sediment.

The comfort of Rome was well behind us, but none of us thought of it much. It was as though we had come from a pleasant holiday, and now we were back on our jobs in a place where we might be needed, and we were Unit 319 again, ready to go to work.

The curfew in Florence was at ten, and our performances were given at two in the afternoon, in a theater that was not the best in the world to play in. It had been picked for us by two enthusiasts who had been carried away by its seating capacity, which was three thousand. But it had been designed for motion pictures and had more length than breadth and no acoustic properties whatever. We mastered it, in time, but our vocal cords knotted in outrage at the demands made on them, and we envied Flush who didn't have to worry about being heard.

"I know," said Brenda, "but he worries about being seen. Those back rows are so very far away."

Kit was terribly distressed at thinking that it might be difficult for the men out front. More than ever she wanted them to be relaxed and distracted, because these were the combat men, down with eight hours' leave and a ticket to the B.O.W.S. distributed at the front.

We learned the look of men just come from combat, something that we could recognize anywhere afterwards. It was a gray look, drawn and empty, as if they had dug themselves out of their own graves. We wondered how they could sit through a play, but they did, and when they laughed we felt as though they had given us a present. And when they came back to see us they gave us actual presents. The Fifth Army wears scarves instead of ties, red for the engineers, blue for the infantry, and soon all our throats blossomed with them, making us feel that we belonged just a little to these men who were so wonderful.

We saw them back-stage and we saw them in the hospitals. The allied casualties were about ten thousand a week, and the stretchers seemed never to stop coming. The men lay in that same way with their faces averted, just as they came from the field stations, their muddy boots hanging over the stretcher edges, beside them their pocket things: a knife, a wallet, a package of cigarettes, a stick of chewing gum, the small things of their only tangible world.

In one of these lines we saw a boy in hopeless, soundless tears. McKay Morris took his hand. "Look, son," he said, "I wouldn't do that. There are a lot of men here that need a lot of courage, and you've got to help them. You tell me what you're up against, and I'll stick around and see you through it." Kay stayed with him till he had to go to the theater, and after the performance he rushed from the villainies of Edward Barrett back to the hospital. The boy had been operated on and when he came out of the ether Kay was standing by his cot. "Hi, Mac," he said as if to a pal, and went peacefully to sleep again. Emily told us about this, and we thought that that was Kay's citation. He and Emily were magnificent in the hospitals; they had a way of bringing confidence, and the men called them Red and Mac. They were permitted in wards closed to the rest of us, though only Kay had been with the badly burned. They never spoke, he said, but looked out at him from a terrible silent place of their own. It was as if they thought that our world was no longer theirs, and that we could never understand what theirs was. "Go away," they seemed to implore him. "Go away, laugh, have a drink, but leave us in our limbo."

We stayed three and a half weeks in Florence. It rained, and the Arno was turgid, with a smell as heavy as death. The military traffic pushed forward with men and supplies, rattling back empty the next day for more, thick with the mud that is Italy's own, dense and gluey and slippery as axle-grease, adding to the desolation about us. I could remember a Florence of villas and gardens and a life that shared the sophistication of a city with the charm of the country. Now despair had touched everything. The people tramped stockingless in worn-out shoes; their faces were paper-white with cold and hunger, and their suffering seemed to emanate from their bones. There was hunger in the south, too, but here it was desperate.

Rome and the illusion of normalcy might have been a mirage. The palaces along the Lungarno were windowless and crumbling. In sparing the Ponte Vecchio, the Germans had still wanted to make it useless for military traffic and had blown up two blocks on each side, and two blocks in depth, and there was nothing left but peaks of rubble. I saw an old woman sitting on one of these. It was a heap of flowerpots and cement, bits of blue glass, a mangled shoe, twisted cooking things, odds and ends of clothing, all the torn fragments of a house and God knows how much humanity. But she stayed there and every now and then she would poke at it unseeingly, as if touch might recreate a home. The privation was everywhere, but there was nothing to do and we could only turn away, back to ourselves and our own concerns.

Now the chief one was Betty's wedding. The waiver for Bob Hester had come through. Our beloved Ed Comm at Caserta had taken a hand, as fatherly as Betty could have wished for, and the wedding day was set. And for the moment we were less the B.O.W.S. and more the family of the bride. Betty hadn't got the parachute silk and was hunting for a wedding dress. Brenda was deep in concocting a hat. She was also trying to reconcile Flush to Sergeant Voight, who was still with us. His chief had a Santa Claus heart, and had detailed the sergeant to three weeks of guarding his wife, and everyone was pleased but Flush.

"I don't understand Treasure," said Brenda. "I thought he would like to see me happy."

But Treasure thought not, and continued to bite Sergeant Voight whenever he saw him, which was all the time.

A day or so before the wedding we went to a party. Brian had met a colonel of the Argyle and Sutherlands who had a lot of Scots back in the hills, all in from the front for a three days' rest. They had lost half their buddies and their spirits were low, and they wondered if we would go and see them.

"They'll have a big fire, and a hot dinner, and we'll sit around and talk to them and cheer them up a bit," said Brian.

We couldn't see why not, and at five of a chilly evening we started off. Brian, Bob, and me, Erik, Roger, Elaine, Guthrie, Emily, Brenda, Gert, and McKay.

We had been warned that it would be a long trip and close to the front, but as one hour passed to a second one I began to get restless and hungry. The road was full of bomb craters and signs that said, "Mines: keep to the middle, sides not cleared." I was sure our driver would see them, but as the car lurched from side to side, I read them aloud, just in case. Emily Lawrence was enjoying it. "It's rugged," she said; "it's good for us; we've all had it too soft lately." At that the car hit a bump and we rose in our seats, hitting our heads sharply on the roof with the unanimous precision of Rockettes.

"I hope that was rugged enough for you, Emily dear," I muttered through my pain.

Brenda tried to soothe us with talk of the wonderful dinner we would have. "Wild turkey and apple and onion stuffing."

I said peevishly that there were no onions in Italy.

"Nonsense, dear," said Brenda. "Every one of them will have been sent onions from Scotland. And there'll be sweet potatoes and white potatoes and a very special sort of cheese."

"Oh, shut up, Brenda," said Guthrie, saving me the trouble.

I knew Brenda was indulging in fantasy, but I couldn't help seeing a stuffed turkey right in front of me, and I drooled in anticipation. We bumped along, and about when I had decided that we would spend the night on the road and only Emily would be happy, there was one last jerk and we were there. Colonel

Graham came to meet us. "Thank God you're here," he said; "the men have been waiting an hour for the show to begin."

"The show!" gasped Brian. We had never thought of a show. We thought we were coming to dinner, and Brian was about to say so, but he stopped when he saw the pains that had been taken for us. There was a mound about four feet high, and a tarpaulin had been stretched on it, and on each side two trucks sent their headlights through the misty night to give illumination. There was even a timid, moist piano. And sitting on the grass were about two hundred and fifty Jocks.

"We can't disappoint them," I said to Guthrie, "but where's my turkey?"

"I think we've brought it with us," said Guthrie, "and it will be our little show."

The colonel took us to a small whitewashed farmhouse and we gulped tea and sandwiches while Brian hastily arranged a program. He would be master of ceremonies and Roger would play, and Elaine and Brenda would sing. We hurried back to the trusting Jocks and Brian introduced himself and told all the jokes he could think of. The Jocks laughed happily. "Oh, look now," they would repeat after each one. Elaine Perry sang, and the headlights shone on her red hair and picked out the green behind her, and I thought how lovely she looked.

The piano was an apologetic wreck, with half the keys mute, but Roger skipped manfully around them, and the Jocks beat time to the playing. From the hills I heard a rumbling. "Thunder?" I whispered to Brian. "Artillery," he told me. "You can see the gunfire from the mound."

Brenda sang, and then Brian introduced the rest of us. I had my candy ration with me, and since I couldn't do anything else, I tossed it out to the men, feeling a bit silly, but the Scots get very little sweets and it turned out to be a welcome gesture.

We had done all we knew how to, but the Jocks had no idea of ending the party, and there was an anxious pause. Then Colonel Graham said that they ought to entertain us for a while, and we joined the audience on the grass. Beyond the little stage we heard piping, and then up into the light came the three regimental pipers, carefully balancing their square-booted feet till they stood in the center. Their belts and their spats were white, and their silver buckles shone and they piped till they piped us away from Italy into a Scottish glen. A major began to sing.

> If it's thinking in your inner heart braggarts in my step
> You've never smelt the tangle of the Isles.

He rolled his tongue over the names, Tummel and Loch Rannoch and Lochaber, and the Jocks moaned with homesickness. "Come on, lads," he called to them; "remember it's your turn." We had more songs, and imitations of Harry Lauder by men who were more like him than he was himself.

The Jock beside me kept saying, "Oh, we wish Johnny were here. Oh, but he was gay, he could make you laugh no matter what; he was our real fun guy, but we lost him . . . we lost him."

At the end the major called us back to the mound, and we crossed our hands with those on each side of us till we formed a chain that joined with the men below. From the distance the reverberations and flashes were very clear. Then the pipers came playing "Auld Lang Syne" and we sang it together, faster and faster, till we could no longer hear the booming of the guns.

Back at the farmhouse the room was a warm tangle of firelight and green kilts and rich burring voices. We had sandwiches and hot rum and more piping and a toast in Gaelic which they translated for us: "To our King, and Princess Louise, Duchess of Argyle, and to the present company." Then they disengaged our driver from a bagpipe he was trying to play and waved us off.

All the way back to Florence we hummed the major's song. I was sleepy but I came out of it asking a question.

"What's a braggart in my step?"

"I think it's a burr of some sort," said Brenda. "You know, dear, one of those beastly little things you pick up in the woods."

"No, no," roared Brian. "It's a swaggering walk."

Well, I thought, they have a right to it.

The next days went in a bridal flurry. The wedding plans were made, and all we lacked was a dress for the bride, a hat for Brenda, and the groom, who was still in Foggia. But we didn't worry, because whatever Providence that is in charge of wed-

dings seemed to be keeping a special eye on this one. Colonel Penell, chaplain of the Fifth Army, was going to marry them, and he
had asked if they would like his rectory for the honeymoon. It
was a perfect little house, with a garden and a maid. He warned
them it would be cold, but the lovely living room had an open
fireplace, and he thought they would be all right.

"Even if they freeze," said Brian, "at least they'll be alone."

Betty couldn't get her parachute silk, and was almost recon-
ciled to being married in her uniform, or an ordinary dress, when
a woman in the Red Cross offered her own wedding gown, as
trained and glistening as a bride could hope for. The female
B.O.W.S. sighed with delight when Betty tried it on, and Brenda
disappeared and came back later with a cluster of feathers and
ribbon. "It's my hat, dears," she said. "That dress inspired me.
Now everything is settled."

Everything was settled except the time of the groom's arrival.
The day before the wedding he telephoned that he was in Sienna,
but would have to thumb a ride from there, and wouldn't be at
the rehearsal, and also his best man couldn't get leave, and would
Roger Stearns mind taking his place? Roger was delighted, and
stood up at the rehearsal with Gert Macy who substituted for
the groom, waiting at the altar with dignified restraint while
Guthrie practiced giving the bride away, and the rest of us issued
whatever stage directions occurred to us.

The chapel was white marble with carved figures of saints at
the altar, and the next morning it was full of flowers and sunshine. Bob Hester had arrived, Emily had dressed Betty and now
we were waiting for the organ to tell us she was coming. We
had done the best we could with our appearances and we were
nice and shiny, though Chester Stratton hadn't got his laundry
in time and was wearing a white civilian shirt. This caught Mc-
Kay Morris' eye, and he rebuked Chester. "You're not in uniform," he said, ignoring the brilliant pink scarf knotted round his
own neck.

Colonel Penell was robed and at the altar, and Bob and Roger
came to stand in their places. The sun caught Bob's flying wings,
and his eyes that were so like Betty's were very serious. Then
we heard the familiar chords and we stood and faced the arched

chapel door. Brenda came first, her bouquet gay against her slim dress. She passed us, and her flowers shook a little in her hands. There was a whisper of satin and the arch framed Betty on Guthrie's arm, and our throats tightened.

Her head was up and she looked straight ahead to the boy waiting for her. Emily spread her train and she went like a steady little candle to meet him, and they knelt for the service.

"Who giveth this woman?"

Kit wiped her eyes unashamed. I gritted my teeth.

"Will you, Betty Sue, take Robert Apply . . ."

"It's just a radio serial," I told myself, as Chester Stratton began weeping down my neck. "It's just the adventures of Betty and Bob—it isn't even happening." But I saw my Bob wipe his glasses and I gave up and cried like everybody else.

The organ flung itself into Mendelssohn. We blew our noses under its clamor and followed Lieutenant and Mrs. Hester to the rectory.

Nancy and Brenda had filled it with all the flowers in Florence, dahlias and gladioli and roses. There was a cake and toasts and Betty kept saying, "Where's my husband?" as if he weren't standing beside her holding her hand tightly. And when we left them, they were still standing like that.

"I don't know why you said good-bye to her," Brian said to me going back in the bus; "she'll be seeing us all at the theater, poor girl." But she didn't seem to mind, and it was a very festive performance, enhanced by the arrival of our long underwear. It had been getting steadily colder, and the B.O.W.S. had been shivering, but when we saw the garments unpacked, we weren't sure that Emily wasn't right and a little rugged endurance wouldn't hurt us.

"Mine looks awfully male," I said to Bob.

"It is, dear," he answered. "They couldn't get any other kind." I tried it on and the shirt came to my knees, and the legs bagged loosely, and I looked like a kneeling elephant.

"I won't wear them," I said, but I did, and I was warm but depressed. The shirt drooped under a skirt, and bulged under slacks. I tried tying it around my waist, but it would escape and passing GIs would mention that my slip was showing.

When the elation of the wedding had passed we all felt a little flat, and Kit thought that an expedition might revive us. This seemed a very good time to make a pilgrimage to the home of the Robert Brownings, so one morning a grave little group of us solemnly strolled to the apartment to bend our reverential knees. Outside we read the plaque which tells that the two great poets had lived there, and we hesitated in respect before we knocked.

Those two brave spirits must have left something of themselves in this place where they had been so happy, I thought, and we knocked on the heavy wooden door half expecting that Robert Browning might open it and glare in resentment at Brian. Or maybe Brian would do the glaring, because actors are generally better looking than the characters they play.

But it was not Robert Browning that opened the door. It was a blonde, wearing a kimono and an inviting smile, which changed to amazement when she saw us. We explained what we wanted, and her face fell, but she let us in and showed us through. It was a long dark apartment, with the rooms opening one out of the other. Kit looked at the little room Elizabeth Barrett had used as a study, and then went and stood on the balcony at the end of the flat, unable to say a word.

Brian, however, ignored the sadness of the present situation and was excoriating the past. "I don't understand the Brownings," he said. "They dig themselves out of that dark, dreary London, and they dig themselves into this dark, dreary apartment! Why, it hasn't even a garden and all it does is look onto another brick wall!"

Nancy and I watched him as he strode up and down. "But you'll still play the part, won't you?" we asked him, nervously.

It rained again, and the mud was indescribable. Kit went to a hospital very near the front wearing three coats and a raincoat over them and boots to her hips. She said it was like nothing you could imagine; we think of mud as a layer over grass or gravel or asphalt, but this was mud over mud, with nothing else to be seen. And the cold was bitter and the work unceasing. The nurses and the doctors never took their clothes off. They worked, and lay down for a few hours, and got up to work again.

Kit was feeling more and more that our real usefulness was near the front. Seeing what the men came from made her even more convinced. "If it's just to sit and look at something besides mud," she said, "it must help them. It's two and a half hours for them to forget in."

We were to go to Leghorn after Florence, but the day before we were to leave the telephone came into Kit's life again.

We were giving two performances that day, one at two and one in the evening. When we did this Kit stayed in the theater, as by the time she had talked to all the men who came back, there wasn't more than a little while left before the next curtain. There was no way of getting food to her, though, so she used to save something from our lunch mess to make a sandwich. I remember in Florence Nancy had twisted a coat hanger into a species of toaster, and Kit would warm her bread and tuna fish or whatever she could get over a small oil burner that was on the stage.

She was doing this when she was called to the telephone in the theater box-office. General Mark Clark wanted to know if it would be possible on such short notice to take the play to Montecatini where he was setting up a rest camp. It was about ten miles from the front, he said, and they could bring the men down in trucks for a couple of days' rest. This time Kit didn't even gasp. She just said "Yes," and Leghorn was postponed and we were in Montecatini in twenty-four hours.

CHAPTER ELEVEN

TEN MILES from the front sounded as though we might be going to play in some abandoned village in a theater improvised from a schoolhouse or church, with our speeches lost in the sounds of battle. But Montecatini had been a fashionable spa and was large and infested with hotels and small marble temples where chic notables had fluttered to sip the waters. There had been smart little restaurants and shops and parks and all the appurtenances of a time when taking the cure was part of the social season. Now the restaurants were boarded up and the parks were a maze of slit trenches, and we might have been on a movie set in California for all the battle sounds we heard. Occasionally from behind a far-off hill we saw a puff of smoke, but that was all.

Our hotel was steaming with activity and filled with packing cases of food, and in the office we found an actor friend, Edmund Trevor. I had last seen him in the play *Valley Forge* as the handsome young Lafayette; now he was attending to the organization of this huge rest camp. As soon as possible, he said, there would be clubs and movies and a whole program of recreation was planned, but they had only been at it three days and the town was no more than set up, which meant, principally, light, water and food. But already the men were pouring in, brought down from the front in truckloads, and we watched as they piled into the courtyard where Italian boys were waiting with tubs of water.

First they scraped the mud from the heavy high boots with knives, and then the men stood in the tubs, and the boys washed the boots down, then the men streamed into the hotel. Here was the combat look again and though we knew they were young, they were so tired and spiritless and dazed they might have been any age. They nearly all brought a bottle of vino with them, and they sat with it in the hotel lounge and listened to the band that played there.

They were completely on their own, as General Clark had given instructions that they were not to be policed. Rape and bottle throwing were out, but otherwise the MPs were to leave them alone.

But though they had this freedom, they didn't seem to know what to do with it. Some of them wandered in the streets, and sometimes a fight would spring up, and they would slug away for a while, and as suddenly lose interest and stop and walk away. Some of them just went to sleep wherever they happened to be, and the hotel lobby was full of sprawled men, as limp and forlorn as our piles of equipment.

They were desperately weary and heavy with strain and they looked starved for rest and distraction. Some of the doubts we had had at Caserta came back to me, and I found myself wishing we really were a show, full of light and color and music.

As we went to the theater they were strolling the streets restlessly, and occasionally a helmet would be tossed from a hotel window in an irritated way.

"They'll never come to the Barretts," I was certain.

But there was a good line waiting for the performance, though it eyed us a bit grimly as we went by.

"Who are they?" asked one. "Movie actresses?" His buddy considered my slacks and trench coat. "I wouldn't know," he said. "They look like GIs to me."

The theater was large, and our dressing rooms were scattered, but McKay Morris had one near mine. "I don't like it," he said as he was making up. "I don't like it. This time I'm really scared. Most of those boys have bottles and they're all good shots."

"They're not allowed to throw bottles," I told McKay, but I remembered those helmets coming out of windows and I didn't like it either, and I couldn't help feeling glad I had only a small part to play, a very unusual state of mind for me, or any other actress.

It felt more and more like Caserta, especially when Guthrie came to give all of us a kind word and check on our spirits. I thought his own were a little shaken. "Well," he said, "I had a cheery little message on my mirror." Actors on tour often write messages in greasepaint on the mirror for any friends that may be following the next week—"Darling Maurice, hope Pittsburg loves Hamlet." That sort of thing. But Guthrie's message had a different flavor. It was dated a month back and it read: "To you God damn British and Americans—we're leaving now but we'll be back. Heil Hitler!"

Before the curtain went up we could hear the men out front, their heavy boots scraping down the aisles, and helmets rolled like garbage cans in an alley.

The curtain went up and the play started and at first there was no particular reaction one way or another, but as the act progressed we began to be conscious of a voice in one of the boxes, monotonous and continuous. Kit tried to ignore it, but it got louder and all of a sudden it burst into the assertion that the Thirty-fourth Division was the best goddamned division in the whole goddamned Army.

"I hope you don't find the room very close, Mr. Browning?" said Kit on the stage to Brian who had just entered.

"The Thirty-sixth is the best!"—came from the opposition, and a fine loud argument began while Kit and Brian went doggedly on.

"I'm afraid it would be quite useless my trying to play-act with you," said Kit as Elizabeth Barrett, thinking she might have to say it in reality, but a major in the audience rose and interrupted the debate. "Men," he said, "what *does* it matter?" And silence fell, and they turned into as good an audience as we had ever played to, with only one more incident in the second act, when one of them thought it would be funny to repeat the ends of all our lines after us; but the others shouted, "For God's sake, shut up." "All right, I will," he replied meekly, and went fast asleep.

Afterwards Kit and Brian stayed twice as long as usual shaking hands and talking, because not just some of them but the entire houseful of men came back-stage in a body. One of the first was the boy who had started the discussion in the box. He went straight to Kit and apologized. Then he dug down in his pocket and brought out a religious medallion that he had carried for thirty-six months, and gave it to her. We watched their faces as they came back, and it was wonderful to see that some of the strain was gone. They were friendly and good-natured and we felt that maybe we had been a step in the adjustment of these men who had seen ninety-six to one hundred and thirty-six days of continuous fighting, and we knew definitely that this was the theater's real function with the army.

That night Kit got her most cherished compliment. As they left us Gert heard one say to another, "Didn't I tell you this'd be better than a whorehouse?"

When we had arrived there were about three thousand men in Montecatini; when we left it was nearer thirty thousand. We would wake to hear the trucks unloading in the courtyard, at three and four in the morning. They were bringing them down under cover of darkness now, as lines of trucks invited strafing, and the roads were risky in the daylight.

They still sat in the lounge, and Roger Stearns would play for them when the band was off duty, and Betty and Emily and Elaine would dance with them, but they were only three and often we would see the men sadly dancing together. It was getting near time to think of Christmas presents and they would stare in the windows of what shops were open, trying to find something to send home. There was very little to choose from, strings of cheap beads and souvenirs and picture postcards that leaned heavily on vulgarity for humor: "The waters of Montecatini are very relaxing," with appropriate illustration, and the GIs snorted in disgust. There was a bookstore, but all the books, naturally enough, were in Italian. But they bought what things they could and took their purchases to the Red Cross to be wrapped. I had found a few things myself, and I stood waiting in line with them. The man back of me had a baby's dress and some beads. I told him they were pretty. "They're not as nice as I'd like, ma'am, but we only get a few hours for shopping before we go back to the hills."

"Those hills!" said another. "They tell you to take the darn thing and you bust yourself doing it, and when you get it, what have you got? You've got two hundred more hills stretching ahead of you!"

"It's better than standing around freezing," said another, cheerfully. "It's a great life, ma'am—you're either bored to death or shot to death."

They asked where the Barretts were going next. I told them Leghorn and then France.

"Oh, boy," they said, "the fashionable front." When I left the line they waved to me. "Don't forget this old forgotten front when you get to Paris." I wanted to tell them that we would never forget, and that the truth was that none of us wanted to leave at all. We had got to know them very well at the hotel where we were billeted together—we knew all the symptoms and phases of their fatigue, and we thought we understood them. We learned to pick our way through menacing arguments knowing that they would lead to nothing more than a shared bottle of vino. We listened to their vividly decorated arraignments of Brass and Italy and C rations and mud. We had got into a few bouts with them ourselves. Brenda came back from the theater one evening to find herself stopped and accused of having been out with Brass. Brenda tried to explain that she had been working at the theater, but this was brushed aside. She could be out with Brass, too, couldn't she? Some said yes and some said no and there was every indication of a fight starting.

"Gentlemen," said Brenda in her most clipped British accents. "You wouldn't fight before an American gell!" "No," they cried, and fell into each other's arms.

"It was all I could think of to stop it," said Brenda. "And I *have* taken out my first papers."

Sometimes they were blindly aggressive, as if they were trying to find their own identity again, and could only do it through assertion.

One of them seized a handful of a sweater Bob was wearing and twisted it. "Take it off," he said. Bob struggled out of it, and gave it to him, but he flung it back.

"I don't want your goddamned sweater," he said, almost sobbing. "I want to fight. Why do you have to be so goddamned nice about it."

"Don't pay any attention to Red," said one of his friends. "He's had a tough time. He's really a good guy." It ended with Red talking to Bob for three hours straight. "Thanks," he said at the end. "I was going nuts."

Some of them came out of their fatigue fairly quickly. Sleep and being clean had an almost immediate effect. Some of them seemed to be still sleepwalking in a nightmare of recollection. Some of them were just dulled and acquiescent. But they were all good guys, and we wanted to stay with them and we wished we could play up the lines with them on the end of a truck, though when I said so to a boy back-stage he shook his head. "It's nice seeing the scenery and the stage," he said; "makes you feel more like you're home again."

We still wore our Fifth Army scarves, which had made us feel a little that we were part of it, but before we left Montecatini we were given something that made us feel we really belonged.

One matinee we had a visit from General Clark himself. "At the end of the play I'm giving you the Fifth Army citation," he said, and handed us each a Fifth Army patch.

"Have we really the right to wear this?" we asked.

"You have if I say so," he told us, smiling, and when we proudly assembled on the stage after the performance he gave us the citation:

> *The Barretts of Wimpole Street* is awarded the Fifth Army plaque for exceptionally meritorious service, during the period of 14th October to 10th November, 1944. During this period the distinguished cast of this history-making production, in a manner befitting the artistry of its members, presented performances which were attended by thousands of Fifth Army troops. The memorable entertainment provided by the members contributed materially to the enhancement of the morale of the Fifth Army troops.

Then he made a speech and said that the Fifth Army plaque was given for excellence in discipline, performance and merit. He said he had been sure about two of these, but didn't know about a third. "However," he said, "when I called Miss Cornell, and the whole company was here and ready to work in twenty-four hours, I knew that as well as performance and merit, they had discipline, too."

I think that made us proudest of all, and there was braggart in our steps for quite a while afterwards.

We hated to leave Montecatini, and we hated to leave Italy. We had one last performance in Leghorn, and we all stood on the veranda of the hotel and watched the sun set.

"We've been in Italy seventy-nine days and played seventy-eight performances," said Kit.

"And eleven cities," said Gert. "We'll be in another war zone tomorrow; we'll be ETOUSA now."

"Can we still wear our Fifth Army patch?" I wanted to know. Betty said nothing. She was holding tight to her husband's hand; she would be saying good-bye to him the next day, as he and Freddy Voight were both leaving us.

We could see the Island of Elba against the brown and crimson sky, and we watched it till it melted in the fading light. Moths began to flutter past us, and it was time to go to bed, but we lingered, looking out to the direction of France.

The gorgeous sunset of the night before was forgotten in the icy dawn of our departure. We were getting hardened to flying, but we hadn't had any bad weather, and now it looked ominous. But we got obediently into our plane, only to get out as obediently a few seconds later. "One engine's busted," said our pilot through the loud-speaker. "We'll change to another plane."

"Well, it's nice to have found it out now," said Nancy as we made for another ship. Just as we were getting in we saw a small plane land and turn over and over, rather gaily, I thought.

Our crew watched it indifferently. "It's an Eyetie, busting up one of their own planes. They bust up everything."

Somebody cared, however, because we were relieved to see a small ambulance go tearing over to its assistance. We would have liked to know just what had happened to it, but we were taking off.

It was only a little after six in the morning and very cold. We spread army blankets over our knees, and Brian had a knitted cap and his pipe and looked like Sherlock Holmes. Kit and Nancy had scarves knotted under their chins, and each had a book. I looked at the titles, and looked quickly away again. They were *Blood on the Snow* and *Coffins for Two*.

The loud-speaker addressed us. "In case this trip is bumpy, folks, take the liners out and use your helmets."

We removed the liners at once and it started to be bumpy at once. "We can't get above the storm; we're flying low but it won't be bad long," said Guthrie, encouragingly.

And there was a sudden wild lurch and everyone was on my side of the plane at once yelling "Look!" And there were two enormous waterspouts a thousand feet high, and their spray must have risen a thousand feet more, and there was another forming in a whirlpool that immediately rose into a huge column of water.

"Poor Billy Rose," I said through the green and purple juices already concentrating in my throat; "it's much better than the Aquacade."

We may have flown out from under the storm, but Guthrie was wrong about its getting better; it got very much worse, and I retreated into a haze of complete misery, shared by almost all the rest of us. Elaine and Emily and Guthrie and McKay were infuriatingly undisturbed, and even interested in scenery. "France!" they exclaimed at one point and piled over me to gaze out of my window. "Why does everything have to be on my side of the ship?" I said, pushing them off again.

That was the end of my resistance and I collapsed, but I was not alone. Bob was lying full length on the floor, Erik and Roger had buried their heads in their arms, and McKay Morris' lap was filled with the heads of the seedy, and he waved to me as much as to say, "Standing room only." But at last we began to come down. We pulled ourselves together, staggered to our feet and tumbled thankfully out of the plane onto the wrong airfield.

"Oh, God," we said, when George Keane broke the news to us, and we knew we had to start off again. But it was only twenty minutes more and not long after that we were on our way to Marseilles, our health restored enough for us to stare out from the cars and murmur "France."

"I can't believe I'm here," I said to Bob, when we drew up at the Hôtel Noailles. We got our rooms and went to the elevator and came face to face with a familiar sign: "*Ascenseur ne marche pas.*"

"I believe it now," I said as we climbed to the fourth floor.

CHAPTER TWELVE

BAEDEKER throws up its hands in despair at Marseilles and says: "There is absolutely nothing of any interest here." But Baedeker hadn't been in war-torn Italy for three months, and didn't know that a kiosk that sold newspapers in French and English was a fascinating sight, or that sprays of mimosa in November could be irresistible. And probably it didn't think of Jean's bar in the Hôtel Noailles where we could sit and sip good French cognac and say "Hi!" to the British and American soldiers and sailors who strayed in and out.

Civilians came too, and the women were a sight in themselves with their hair piled into puffs and curls and surmounted by mountainous hats.

We may have been as strange a sight to them, because our own wardrobes were now reduced to a pair of slacks, a skirt and jacket, three shirts, three pairs of underwear, two of which we always wore, so that we bore out the GI term for us, which was "round actors."

The old port had been pulverized by German demolition bombs, but the hotel was intact and pleasant and unexpected people were always cropping up. Our own Tommy Ewell, whose ship was now in Toulon, and Anne O'Hare McCormick, on her way to Italy.

Clare Boothe Luce, also Italy bound, had dinner with us, looking fresh and young and orderly and energetic, qualities that I have always admired in her since we met when I played in *The Women*.

"What do you think of the appearance of the French-women?" she shot at me journalistically.

All I had seen of France so far was Marseilles, which is hardly a sartorial criterion, and I said so. "I can't judge by Marseilles; it's like Bridgeport, Connecticut."

This made her rather stiff. "You forget I represent Connecticut," she said, turning into Congresswoman Luce.

When we left the dining room she picked up my half-smoked package of cigarettes and a celluloid case. "I'll take these," she said. "I love scrounging, don't you? Do you know there are ethics about it?"

I said I hoped not, that would ruin it. "You mustn't come over here with your fancy ideas and spoil our old-fashioned fun," I said as I bade her good night and wished her a safe trip.

"No," she said. "If you take something you must give something back in return." And that night I found a pair of pink wool pants waiting for me, my most valued possession from then on.

While we had been bouncing about in the air, our scenery had been put on a boat to follow us, and was expected to arrive in about four days. Bob and Bill Noon thought they would use some of the time in going to Cannes to check on the theater and see if it would be possible for us to play there. It sounded a pleasant jaunt, so Erik Martin, Chester Stratton, Brian and Brenda and I went along. Gert gave us an almost motherly farewell. "Just don't let anything happen, children," she said. "The minute the scenery gets here we start working."

The drive was long, but it was a lovely soft day, and the road was deserted. "When you think of the Hispanos and Isottas and Rolls that used to streak down to the Riviera," said Brian, nostalgically.

Now we passed only a few jeeps and soldiers and Goums. Goums are Moroccan natives and citizens of France and they wear long sheepskin robes and carry daggers in their belts.

Chester Stratton had been gazing dreamily at the countryside lost in a nostalgia of his own. "Have you noticed the French toilet paper," he said. "I think they make it out of old razor blades."

We passed through Saint-Raphaël which still bore witness to the destruction of the invasion; the Germans had built a huge sea wall, and there were pill boxes and gun emplacements everywhere. Most of the villas had been smashed by artillery fire, and the approach to the beautiful curving beach was littered with the skull and crossbone signs that said: *"Achtung:Minen."*

We were billeted at the Hôtel Carlton in Cannes and we went to sit on the terrace. The Riviera had suffered from lack of food perhaps more than any place in France. At least, any place that we saw. The food supply was dependent on transportation and as there had been none, the people had literally starved. Later I saw a small tin of milk that had cost ten dollars, and a cake of soap that cost five, and biscuits at forty cents apiece. GI supplies, bought in the black market. At the Martinez Hôtel officers in the Army and Navy were allowed to bring one guest at dinnertime, and the lobby was filled at this hour with girls of fifteen and sixteen and seventeen who waited to be picked up in the hope of a meal.

There was a GI joke that the only approach you needed to a girl was *"Voulez-vous diner, avec moi?"* but it wasn't much of a joke when you saw that most of these girls were not the sort that ordinarily could be approached. All of them were very pretty, of course, but too many of them looked simple and sweet.

And yet, against this, on the Carleton terrace there were still a handful of people left over from a passed world. The women wore high platform shoes which we learned cost one hundred and fifty dollars a pair, although their clothes were plain enough. But they had the papier-mâché look of pleasure seekers in their faces, and they were drinking cocktails that cost two dollars. A girl came by in a French peasant costume and offered tiny sandwiches from a tray.

Brian took one, and the girl said, "A dollar, please." And Brian quickly put it back on the tray. "For the starving children of France," she said reprovingly. Brian took the sandwich back again and gave her a dollar. "Why don't they give them those?" he said.

Why didn't they give them the money those platform shoes had cost, I wondered, or the two dollars that disappeared down their throats with every martini.

Bob and Bill Noon went off investigating theaters, and the rest of us went to visit a hospital at Cannes which was filled with our wounded from the Southern Italian front. We had heard

there were mostly paratroopers there, and we wondered if we
would see any of our friends from that exciting night at Capua,
and extraordinarily, we did.

Ranier, who had sung their song for us, had been killed they
said; Phil Huston had been smashed up and was in a hospital.
Captain Johnny Gray was training new men somewhere. It was
wonderful to see them again, and we were glad the hospital was
such a fine one. It had been a tuberculosis sanitarium and every
room opened onto a porch where they could lie in the sun.

We drove on to Nice to pick up Bill and Bob, and saw the
incredible job of camouflage the Germans had done. They had
painted out the town so that from the sea or a plane it looked
half its size, they had painted false roads so that a tank landing
from the sea would run right into a gun emplacement, and
sprinkled prettily on the roads were rose-covered cottages with
white curtains at their windows, concealing the pursed mouths
of howitzers.

We wanted to see Maxine Elliott's villa, but it had been so
heavily mined no one dared step on the grounds. We wanted to
see Monte Carlo but that was off limits to all Allied troops.
However, we saw Josephine Baker in a French naval uniform
and a Fiji Island headdress, and we saw Isabel Pell.

Lieutenant Baker's record as an entertainer was a high one,
and Isabel Pell had entertained too, in her own way. She had
delivered forty-seven Germans to the American colonel on Invasion Day and she was going to have a street named after her.

"Pell Mell, probably," said Brenda, "and a good name, too."

We were ready to leave when Gert telephoned us in some irritation. The scenery hadn't come, she said, and we could take our
time driving back.

We headed for Toulon, to call on Tommy Ewell. He gave
us lunch at his mess, and took us down to his ship afterwards,
and we watched German prisoners, who were in the custody of
the French, unloading the flour. They looked like dregs of men,
and they stopped sometimes to scoop up flour that had sifted
into the cracks of the dock, and ladled bilge water into it from
a tin cup and ate it.

As I watched them a lieutenant beside me spoke. "Don't feel

sorry for them," he said; "they're only getting what they gave. This is their own medicine."

"Of course they are hungry," he went on. "They get the same fare they gave the French, a bowl of soup in the morning and a slice of bread at night, and their barracks were built for the French war prisoners by the Germans, and now they are finding out what it's like to live in them."

From the hills there came a loud explosion. "What's that?" I asked.

"That's a mine," said Tommy. "There are millions of them up there that the Germans planted; people step on them all the time."

"And they'll be doing it for years," said the lieutenant as he looked down at the prisoners working below. "I'd like to give them the job of demining."

We drove back to Marseilles in a sunshine that Cézanne might have painted, and I saw a man planting geraniums, and it seemed a hopeful thing to be doing. I hadn't seen a hopeful civilian for a long time, I thought.

Gert met us in Marseilles in a state of suppressed fury. All the ships of the convoy had arrived except the one that had our scenery on it. It had hit a hurricane and stuck on a rock off Corsica. We asked why it couldn't be pushed off.

"They don't dare," said Gert, looking contemptuous of such weakness. "It's loaded with ammunition and our only hope is that it floats off."

"We shouldn't have come to France," said Bill Noon. "I can handle Italian, but French don't make no sense to me, and now look what happens."

"What are we going to do?" we wailed. Gert said that for one thing we were going to play at the hospital in Aix. "Without our scenery?" we asked. "Without scenery or costumes," said Gert.

If we were going to be held up in Marseilles it looked as though we were all going to take it lying down, because now all the colds and coughs and sinus troubles that we had suppressed came out into the open. We rallied for the performance at the hospital, but we were a wheezy group. The stage was a raised platform, with three steps leading up to it on each side, and there was a small room at the left where we waited between entrances. The hospital had provided a sofa for Kit, harder even than her regular one and of a peculiar shape, and there was no curtain so she had to just walk on and adjust herself to it in full view of the audience, and she and Brian had to unfold themselves from the fast embrace that ended the second act and saunter off the platform arm in arm. It was an odd performance, all of us in our olive drab uniforms, Elizabeth Barrett reclining in a shirt and army blouse instead of a trailing gown, drinking porter from a lily cup instead of a silver tankard, holding a piece of Kleenex in lieu of a lacy handkerchief, while Robert Browning swung a trench coat from his shoulders instead of a sweeping cape. Flush was the only one who looked as usual, and it all might have been very funny but the sight of men in the audience with cages covering the stumps of their missing feet and our own struggles with fits of coughing halted any mirth in us.

When it was over Kit felt so ill that they persuaded her to stay in the hospital. Guthrie and McKay Morris were the only healthy Barretts left, and McKay announced that he was going on a hospital train to bring back wounded from the front. "They say they can use me to help carry them on and off," he said and left. Guthrie would have gone with him, but Guthrie was going back to America. The play he was committed to produce couldn't be put off any longer, and he was going on the first plane that would take him. Lieutenant Henry Dudley of the Navy took a look at me and said: "I swear and declare you look peaked!" and took me to the naval clinic, and there I was booked for daily treatments. All the rest of us went continuously to one clinic or another, except Gert who sublimated her own cold in a steady assault on Army channels in the interest of our scenery. In the Army we had learned that channels are essential. At first the word made us think of a rough sea trip, or a far-away island, but this is not the Army definition. Army channels are methods and the protocol for them. The private goes to the corporal, the corporal to the sergeant and so on up, and it involves a great deal of tact and touchiness, because a channel gets awfully hurt if it is skipped on the way to a higher one, and the whole thing is as dependent on observance as a chain letter. But red tape is only a red flag to Gert and she took a Herculean step that landed her right into top Brass.

She also appealed to the Navy and the Airforce, and if the Marines weren't called in it was because they were too busy in the Pacific, not because she didn't think of them, and Brenda, who shared her room, said it was exactly like sleeping in an office, and that the telephone operators referred to Miss Macy as "*la dame qui parle*."

She brought daily bulletins to our sick rooms, of varying promise. One day the Navy was going to push the boat off the rocks, very carefully, of course, so that it wouldn't explode in their faces. The next day the Army had promised to unload the scenery from the ship and fly it to us. But towards the end of the second week of waiting it looked as though the Marines would have to come back from the Pacific, or else Gert would have to swim out herself, and float it back piece by piece, which she was almost ready to do.

Thanksgiving came and went, celebrated by turkey served to us in the seclusion of the servants' dining room of the Grand Hôtel Noailles, and any that were well enough went to the hospital at Aix to do the revue. Kit had had to have a sinus operation and was still in bed. And all the time our scenery stayed rocking, and we hoped gently, on a Corsican reef.

While it stayed there we were forced to inactivity, and perhaps because of it, or because of our colds, or a combination of both, we became swollen with homesickness. Bob and I would talk about Beekman Place, and try to imagine what was happening there. What time was it there? We were six hours ahead. What would our friends and families be doing? It grew, till it became part of the sound of the wind and the rain, and we felt a kinship with the look on the faces of the soldiers in the streets and the men in the hospitals. It was terribly strong and terribly futile, and we tried to disentangle ourselves from it. But it was like any other germ that we had been exposed to, only there are no shots for homesickness, and some of us had it pretty badly.

It might have been better if we had given ourselves up to it, but unfortunately we tried to be little soldiers about it, and it acted on us like measles that turn in, and instead of a good healthy rash of emotion we had an ingrowing irritation that did odd things to our dispositions.

Then, what small self-control we had left was shaken out of us by the wind which became a mistral, and tore at us when we went to the clinics, and when we were indoors took the shutters and windows in its teeth and worried them.

Molehills became the proverbial mountains, and one particular molehill was the PX where we did our weekly shopping for cigarettes, candy, matches and such things. Kleenex was now our greatest need, and the supply was low and erratic, and if one of us appeared with a box when the rest of us had none we felt we had been cheated willfully and with dire purpose, and sulked or raged according to our natures. Nancy, who had stayed even-tempered and sensible through it all, would try to laugh us out of it, and Gert's invariable plea was "For the good of the seventeen," but most of us, and especially me, were deaf to any such high-minded reasoning and continued to glower until the morning that Gert came with the news that the ship was off the rocks.

"Who did it?" we wanted to know. "The Army, the Navy, or the Air Corps?"

"God," said Gert. "It just floated off as calmly as though I had never raised a telephone. It will be here in two days, so pull yourselves together, kiddies."

So—we blew our noses, cleared our throats, and our colds seemed to vanish, and our homesickness and our vapors with them. I guess that's how the GIs feel, I thought; they only gripe when they have nothing else to do.

Kit came back to us from the hospital, and we had to say good-bye to Guthrie. Our never-failing Ed Comm had been able to get a place on a plane, though secretly Guthrie had been hoping he couldn't. He didn't want to go; his experiences on our tour, and in the camps and hospitals, had touched him too deeply. "All I want to do is come back," he kept saying, which anyone who has once played over there understands.

There was only one alleviation for him as he got in the plane. "Gert's going to envy me," he said, waving the list of addresses he had collected of wives and families and sweethearts. "I've got two hundred and sixty-three telephone calls to make."

We opened at last to our first audience in France, and it was a shock to find the references to Italy received in a normal apathy. Bob, who had become accustomed to more or less stopping the show with a line that described Italy as a grossly over-rated country, was quite furious when he got nothing but a cough or two instead of a round of applause.

Kit, however, was stunned by an ovation for a speech that had passed unnoticed in Italy. "We shall be able to get all we need in Paris," she said, and the theater rocked with the GIs' informal interpretation of it.

Otherwise the play went about as usual, and we were happy to be at our job again. The scenery hadn't suffered from its experience and the only casualty was a sweater of Gert's that had been eaten by rats and came out of her barracks bag like confetti, and Brian found that he had packed his flash with the light on and it had been faithfully blazing away in the darkness of his bag. When he took it out, it turned a dim red eye on him and expired. "Well done," said Brian to the battery which had loyally survived to die in its master's hand.

With the return of our normal dispositions we began to take an interest in the things around us again, and in each other. We were all proud of Betty who had been so quietly plucky in her first separation from her husband. I wanted to tell her how much I admired her, but I never could. I passed her dressing room every night when I went to the stage for my last scene, and I would see her sitting at her dressing table looking at the three snapshots of Bob Hester that were propped against her mirror.

"It's not easy to be separated," I said one night.

"But we're never separated," she said simply, "not for a minute."

Outside the theater various things entertained us.

We were amused to learn that Marseilles had watched the erection of the black and white signs of the prophylactic stations and rejoiced because they thought they were going to have a new subway system. When Marseilles learned the truth, it was not only disappointed, but deeply shocked. The whole thing lacked elegance, it was felt.

Chester Stratton had been intrigued by a window display in a shop near the Red Cross, and had memorized it for us. One dirty safety razor, one high buttoned boot with a lift, a mangy brown-gray wig, a tall bottle of bay rum, a short bottle of essence, one rusty straight razor and a pair of shoelaces, all liberally covered with dust and, as Chester said, not cheap either.

Now that we were in France we all wondered if we would get to Paris, which was out of bounds to all Allied troops. But in Marseilles George Keane came to tell us that the ban had been lifted and that we would eventually play there, which was exciting news, but his next piece of information was that we would leave Marseilles for Dijon by train, and we behaved as though we were going to have our first view of the iron horse.

"By train!" we told each other in ecstasy, and started packing our barracks bags in anticipation. I had several new items to add to our usual gas mask and helmets. Tins of grapefruit juice, a couple of tins of cheese, hot-water bottles and our newly acquired pills and nose drops. While I was disposing these so that they wouldn't break and at the same time hoping we wouldn't need them again, Bob came into our room.

"Where have you been?" I demanded. "You look yellow."

"I've been to the clinic," said Bob, "and I've got jaundice, and I *am* yellow." He said they had wanted him to go to the hospital for six weeks. "Will you?" I asked, dreading to leave him behind. But he said he would just stay in bed and get up for the performance, and leave with us the next day.

That departure remains in my mind as the last word in utter confusion. Kit, Nancy, Bob, and I were joined at dinner by two naval friends who had packed a train supper for the entire cast, and somehow, we forgot the time and lingered at the table till George Keane materialized before us in horror and rebuke. "You have seven minutes to catch the train," he said. "Don't you think you had better get started?"

We fell over ourselves down the stairs to the cars, and found that the luggage hadn't been put in. Our train, we thought, our beautiful train! We'll miss it. But the luggage came, and was heaved in on top of us, and then I realized I had lost Bob. "Wait!" I said and started to get out, but Kit pulled me back and slammed the door.

"He'll find us," she said.

I grabbed for the door again. "I won't go without him," I said, but Kit spoke firmly above my protest.

"To the station," she said to our driver, expecting the car to catapult on its way. But it stayed where it was and the driver turned leisurely to look back at us.

"Which station?" he inquired.

"*The* station," said Kit; "there can't be many."

"*I* don't know any but one," said our driver.

"Then go to that," commanded Kit.

I stiffened in my seat, as if by doing that I could hold the car back. "I won't go without Bob," I repeated, and I could almost hear the others think: Then don't.

"I mean it," I said to this unspoken reaction, and someone said that anyone would think I was the only married woman in the world.

"Well," I said loftily, "to me I am."

"Don't worry, Goldie," said Nancy. "When we get there he'll be waiting for us."

The car was speeding along, and when it stopped I was the first one out. There was no Bob waiting for us, and also no station. "Good Lord," Kit groaned, "he's taken us to the railroad yards."

We got back in the car and bumped along and every second seemed endless but at last we found the station.

Soldiers and sailors and civilians were running down the platform shouting in French and English that the train was leaving. Hysterically we hauled out our heavy equipment but there was no one to help us with it.

"We'll never make it," Kit gasped.

"Leave it here, and I will stay with it," I said, "because I'm not going without Bob." But with that a car scraped its brakes and Bob and the Navy came running. "Get on the train," they yelled, "we'll bring the bags."

Kit, Nancy, and I went flying down the tracks. "How'll we

find our car?" I panted, but we couldn't have missed it, because the rest of the Barretts were hanging from its windows like lanterns to guide us.

We were dragged on, and Bob and the Navy staggered after us and heaved the luggage on board. "There's just a bit more—I'll be right back," yelled Bob, and disappeared, and the train gave a disapproving yelp.

I leaned out of a window and shrieked to Bob to hurry, but my voice was swallowed in the misty night. A GI on the platform asked me what my friend's name was. "I've got lungs of iron," he said; "I'll page him for you." I told him it was Bob.

"Bob," he howled, and he hadn't underestimated his lungs. Other people took it up. "Bob," they bellowed till it became a roar."

"Are you Bob?" asked the whole platform at once when he came into sight again with the loyal Navy and the remaining bags. "Yes," he said, spent and more than ever yellow. They seized him and practically carried him to the train that was beginning to move.

"Here he is, ma'am," they yelled, and cast him at my feet. We were off, the platform cheered, and the Navy puffed along beside the speeding carriage.

"Do you always leave like this?" they called after us in echoing awe.

CHAPTER THIRTEEN

NANCY HAMILTON is a girl who takes holidays seriously; there is no nonsense with her about ignoring birthdays or skipping festivals. It was through her efforts that we had turkey at Thanksgiving, and now she was working up to Christmas. We would be in Vittel on the twenty-fifth of December, playing at the hospital there, where there were about three thousand wounded, and we were hardly off the train in Dijon before she started making plans. In Marseilles she had bought three thousand *santons*, to which we had all contributed. The *santon* is the product of a small village near Marseilles, and is a painted figure of a saint, or the Christ child, or Saint Nicholas, and it was Nancy's idea that we present one to each of the men in the hospital, and then sing carols, and afterwards have a party for ourselves. We all wholeheartedly supported the hospital idea, but we were not so sure we wanted anything for ourselves. Our mood wasn't Christmassy; the first rumors of the Bulge had reached us, and we didn't feel like any sort of festivity.

But Nancy was adamant. This was a Christmas we would never have again and we should be together and make it something special and apart.

I consented, though I still felt reluctant, but I went walking in Dijon and gradually a Scrooge-like change took place in me. The air was crisp and there was a Negro United States Army band playing in the square and children in white socks and wooden-soled shoes applauded them as they swung into "The Beautiful Blue Danube." The window displays were pitiful, but there was an air of Christmas in the town. A man passed me dragging a small Christmas tree, and a few twists of red and silver tinsel in a window caused two old women to exclaim with joy and scamper happily down the street. I had an urge to join them, and when I saw a sprig of mistletoe in a flower shop I went in and bought it. From then on I was lost, and I joined a queue of women in front of a toy store, hoping to find ornaments for a tree for General Larkin and Ed Comm, who had been transferred from Caserta, and were here in Dijon, to our immense delight.

The women in the line all carried string bags well filled with carrots and potatoes, and I sighed with relief to think that they could buy them. I hadn't seen any food for civilians to buy since I had been overseas.

The toys in the shop were few, and there was nothing with which to trim a tree. I went all over the little Gothic town, to all the pink- and blue-painted shops, and finally, in a millinery department, I found some colored feathers, and I bought them in red and white and blue, and when the tree was trimmed it looked like the headdress of a circus pony.

But at least I had tried, and I thought that was probably how the people of Dijon were feeling as they made what Christmas effort they could. They were building a small stage in the center square, and when it was done they put life-sized figures of the Holy Family there, to make a crèche for everyone. But they had no lights, and at night it was obliterated, until Bill Noon heard about it, and ran to the theater and liberated some of our equipment and after that the figures stood out in brave relief until curfew under a star of Bethlehem, provided by William Noon of New York and Broadway, and the people of Dijon looked joyfully on their first crèche in five years.

As Christmas got nearer the weather got colder, and back-stage Nancy and Gert laid army blankets on the cement floors of the dressing rooms, and we shared one very small smelly oil stove that we passed from room to room. Elaine Perry called half-hour and fifteen minutes wrapped in a rug, and Flush was held in an army sweater when he wasn't actually on the stage.

My circulation stopped entirely except for one brief moment when a very important letter that I had to carry on to the stage couldn't be found. My cue got nearer and nearer and no one could find the letter; my cue came, and I was about to enter empty-handed when Sergeant Duffy, a very good-looking young man who had been detailed to pull the curtain up and down, came to my rescue and thrust a piece of paper into my hand. Thankfully I took it on and handed it to Emily Lawrence. "Papa sent you this note," I said, and Emily looked at it and said "Oh." Nothing about the Hedleys coming to visit the Barretts which was what she should have said. Nothing about anything, just "Oh." I leaned to look at the paper and read: "3 pr. drawers—long—4 shirts—6 hkfs." Sergeant Duffy had given me his laundry list. Between us, Emily and I stammered out the sense of the note that Elaine Perry wrote out for us every night and on which we had come to depend. We finished the scene, and when I went off I was bright red from nerves, and then I realized I was also warm.

"Did it work all right, ma'am?" asked Sergeant Duffy.

"Sergeant," I said, "it worked beautifully."

But if it was cold in the theater, the hotel was warm enough, and we actually had hot baths when we arrived, which in itself was enough to make Dijon a landmark for me, and the signpost in front of the hotel that read PARIS 210 KILOMÈTRES sent a chill of anticipation down my spine, but not very far from the hotel was the rue Victor Hugo, and I knew General Giraud lived there, and I thought if I could get a glimpse of him Dijon would be complete. Then, through Kit, I lunched with him. Kit and Brian and Gert had called on him the day before, and had been deeply impressed by their visit with him, and he had invited them to lunch the next day. My sigh of envy must have been very apparent, because Kit turned impulsively and said I must go in her place. "Please," she said, "it's a great mistake to try to repeat an experience. I got as much out of my visit today as was possible. Tomorrow could give me no more."

So the following noon I walked with Gert and Brian to the unpretentious house where the General lived.

He was waiting for us in the small sitting room, standing in front of the mantelpiece on which there was a picture of his seven children, three boys and four girls. We asked about this handsome family, and he told us. His voice was rather highly pitched, but his French was slow and clear for our benefit.

His oldest son had been shot by the Germans, his second son was a prisoner, his third captain of a submarine. His wife, he said, and two of his daughters were still German prisoners along with seven of his grandchildren. Another daughter had died during imprisonment in Germany under what he described as "cloudy circumstances." His fourth daughter was in Dijon with him.

We went in to lunch and almost filled the tiny dining room. Gert on his right, across from us Brian, the General's aide, and Mlle. Brée, a fascinating woman, secretary to the French regional commander. I sat at the General's left, and I saw next to his plate one of those linen envelopes that are used in Europe for family serviettes. This one was embroidered with a wreath of blue flowers, and I thought of the picture on the mantelpiece, the four pretty daughters with their hair hanging soft and straight. Which one of them had embroidered this for him, I wondered. Which one of them had died under those cloudy circumstances.

Our lunch was typically French, with Alsatian wine and Chambertin, and through the six courses the General talked to us with great humor and charm. He told how he had made his three escapes, twice from Germany, and once from France when a British submarine took him to Africa, and I wondered, looking at his distinctive intellectual features, his long fine nose, how he had managed not to be recognized.

He told of four attempts on his life, three in Africa and one in France, and that this house we were in was now well guarded.

We talked about Germany and England and America, and he said he had often disagreed with Mr. Churchill, but never with President Roosevelt, though he admitted his first lunch with him in Washington had been somewhat startling, and he described it as consisting of tomato juice, lobster, a glass of milk and a salad, and from his tone we gathered that he had looked on it as being, though unpremeditated, the fifth attempt on his life.

I said how beautiful the food we were eating was, and how happy I had been to see that there seemed to be plenty of it to buy in the shops, and Mlle. Brée told us that fortunately this part of the country had never gone hungry; it was full of vineyards and small farms, and was not dependent on transportation for supplies.

After lunch we went back to the sitting room for coffee, and the General disappeared and returned with a dusty bottle of brandy.

The Germans had occupied the house, and had removed the linen, glassware, and silver, and looted his cellar of his excellent wines. All his library had been taken, too, but he showed us three volumes of Molière illustrated by Bouchier which they had somehow overlooked.

"But this," he said, "is what I cannot understand about the Germans." And he brought us an oil painting and showed us where it had been cut from its frame, and then sewn in again. But first, he said, they had painstakingly filled it with human dung, replaced the backing, and left it to rot.

"I could understand them taking the picture to keep. It is a good one, and they could enjoy it and get some pleasure from it. Or I could understand them slashing it, but to go to so much trouble to commit an obscenity, that I do not understand. And the Germans are a race that pride themselves on personal cleanliness."

When we left Gert thanked him for speaking so slowly for us, and he smiled. "If you haven't the grace to speak the language of your guest, you can at least have the courtesy to speak your own clearly."

We walked back to the hotel, our minds full of his courage and I knew I would always remember those seven lovely children grouped so closely in that picture, and now so irrevocably separated.

The key rack at the hotel had hung accessibly at a side wall, and as we went in and out we hung our keys there or took them from it. When we got back, we saw that it was being changed to the back of the desk, high and not so easy to reach. I asked why, and was told "Security reasons."

I went up to our room where Bob, less yellow but still sick, had to stay except when he went to the theater, and told him. "I wonder what that's for?" he said, and I said maybe because of the rats. He snorted. "Rats don't eat keys," he said. But I was thinking of the trap that always yawned behind the lobby desk, a cage of such immense proportions that I imagined rats to match. "These rats might," I said, and then, telling him about our lunch with the General, I forgot about the significance of keys and security in the Army sense.

But after the play that night, George Keane called us together and we saw that for the first time he was armed.

"From now on," he said, "after dark you will please go about only in groups of four or five, and we have all been instructed to carry firearms, but this of course does not include any of you people. Just keep together, and keep your AGO cards handy."

We had to show them in the hotel when we went back, and also our identification papers, and we realized that the guards around the hotel had been doubled. The faces of everyone were grave and concerned and the voices of the officers and men were pitched to a low key.

"What is it?" we asked. We knew that there was a possibility of bad war news, but very little more.

"The Germans have broken through and attacked our strongest positions, and captured enough material to supply their campaign for the next ten days," we were told. But how did this affect us, we wondered, and were told there was a possibility of raids. Scuttlebutt had it that quantities of paratroopers were being dropped in French and American uniforms. Now we knew why they had changed the key rack to a place where it could be guarded.

We were in possible danger, and our reactions were divided. Mine was not to believe it; others were more serious. Kit's was her invariable one. If it happened, there it was. If it didn't, so much the better; in the meantime, business as usual.

Brenda was among the believers and came tearing to my dressing room with positive proof.

"Don't tell *me* paratroopers haven't been dropped," she said, her eyes blazing. "Look at Treasure."

Treasure was limping, one paw held up, as determinedly pitiful as an illustration of the Little Match Girl.

"He has been stepped on," said Brenda, "and only a German would do it." She gathered him up. "How can he give his performance? He is in agony!"

I said we could carry him through it. "Ah," said Brenda, "but

what about his laugh?" Flush's laugh came in the last act when
Brenda called him and he jumped from my grasp on-stage and
ran off to her with such obvious relief that the GIs shouted.

"Perhaps we could cut it out tonight?" I said, but Brenda
said no. Then, just before I carried him on for that moment,
Brenda took him to one side.

"Flush," she said, "I warn you, if you limp when you make
your exit, I shall come on and pick you up and ruin your laugh.
Those men out front have enough to bear without you bringing
your personal difficulties onto the stage. Now remember, I mean
it." She handed him back to me. "I think he understands," she
said quietly.

He must have, because when his cue came he ran off on all
four feet, and the laugh came as usual.

Once off-stage, he went back to limping, and Brenda took him
in her arms. "The hero," she said. "The little hero!"

"The ham," said Brian. "He didn't want his exit ruined."

The air continued to be spun fine with rumors and some of
the silky strands stuck. Nancy, however, was going valiantly
ahead with her Christmas plans, and paratroopers or no paratroopers, she thought we ought to rehearse our Christmas carols
for the hospital at Vittel, and she assembled us in the mess hall,
with herself as choir mistress, and Roger Stearns at the piano.

First we discussed the selection, with everyone holding out for
a particular favorite and no one even willing to consider a compromise. Then the question of verses came up. Nancy, supported by Elaine and Betty who knew them, thought we should
sing all the verses of each carol. I, who don't know more than
the first verse of any of them, thought that would be enough,
and Kit supported me.

"It's just showing off to sing any more," I said.

"Of course if that's how you feel," said Nancy, and I said it
was, and we began to practice.

"Elaine and Betty will take seconds," said Nancy, looking at
us as if we were the Westminster Choir, "and the rest of you
will carry the air."

Kit said she thought it might be better to keep it simple.

"It will be," said Nancy crisply, "but it has to have form."

She led us off. " 'It came upo-oo-n a midnight clear—' Come on," she said, with the gesture of a Thomas Beecham, and we burst co-operatively into "that glorious so-ong of old." She stopped us. "You're drowning out Betty and Elaine," she said and Betty and Elaine tried not to look smug.

"I think it ought to be simple," said Kit again.

Nancy tapped the piano. "Betty and Elaine take this," she said, and they announced securely and harmoniously that angels bent near the earth to touch their harps of gold.

"Now everyone—" said Nancy, "and come in softly and then crescendo."

"Really," Kit said again, "it should be kept simple."

I said it certainly should.

Nancy's eyelids quivered and closed, and when she spoke there was very little Christmas spirit in her voice. "You weren't asked, Goldie, dear," she said, and I rose haughtily and removed my presence, and went to my own room from where I could hear the voices dwindle and offended footsteps carrying the Barretts one by one to bed, till only Nancy was left singing "God Rest Ye Merry, Gentlemen," in lonely solo, but with not one verse left out.

CHAPTER FOURTEEN

ED COMM came to say good-bye to us as we left for Vittel, our canteens filled with hot water and tucked under our feet to keep them temporarily warm.

"Don't forget to give them the password each day," Ed said to George Keane. "And you know your hotel has been changed, don't you?" We asked why. "Security reasons," said Ed, saluting us in farewell.

Erik Martin turned round to me. "I have just been looking at our map," he said. "Vittel is much nearer the Bulge."

It was also much nearer the North Pole, I thought, when we got to the Hôtel les Tilleurs.

Scenes of beauty fade quickly in my mind, and only a general haze remains, but put me in a dump and I unwillingly record every stick and stone, and the Hôtel les Tilleurs is etched in my memory as indelibly as the tattooing on the breasts of the seamen on our troopship, and would require the same sort of operation to remove.

The main building had a sitting room, like an introduction to a bad dentist, littered with old magazines. There were two small houses at the back bearing the names of the Villa Molière and the Villa Berthe. Kit and Nancy, Brenda and Gert had the rooms on the ground floor of one of them, and Elaine and Betty and Bob and I had two rooms on the second floor. Our room had two beds, one brass and double, the other iron and single, and they so completely filled it that the table wedged between them looked as if it were choking. The wallpaper had faded from some unpleasant color to an unhealthy beige, and the spots on it could have been pattern or grease. There were sagging shutters at the windows, and while there was an outlet for electricity, there seemed to be no bulb or light of any kind, and the temperature was the same as it was outside, which was two below zero.

George Keane escorted us to these igloos, and left us with the information that the mess was three miles away.

"But you'll have transportation to get you there," he added hastily, backing away from our stricken faces.

Bob looked sick and frozen, and I remembered the optimistic last words of the doctor in Dijon. "Be sure he is warm, and see that he doesn't catch cold." So I dug into our barracks bags and got out a ten-dollar electric plate, a bargain we had found in Bari. It never boiled water, but it sometimes warmed it, and I thought I might coax it to an extra effort and make Bob a cup of tea. But Betty and Elaine in the next room also had an electric plate, and the same idea, and, as we plugged in simultaneously, the fuse blew out.

Vittel had been a popular resort, with a combined hotel, casino, theater and ballroom. This was now the hospital, with three thousand of our men in it, where we were to play. It was just across the street from us, and I persuaded Bob to walk over there with me, where one of the doctors checked on him, and suggested that he stay. "He'll be warm and have the right diet," he said. And I thought of the mess three frozen miles away, and it seemed a perfect solution.

When I got back to the Villa Berthe, Elaine and Betty hailed me. Elaine had somehow got some hot water, and they made me a cup of tea, and I held it gratefully in my hands and against my face before I drank it.

The hospital had been warm, I told them; what fuel could be had went to it, so very likely the theater would be warm, too. But when we got there it was icy. The male Barretts had been there early, and done the best they could for us with blankets and stoves, but it was like trying to melt an iceberg with a match.

Bill Noon had been listening to the radio and reported that he had heard Sally. Sally was a German commentator, popular with the GIs, who had christened her the Bitch of Berlin. Her reports of coming events had been phenomenally correct, and Bill said she had promised Vittel a nice little present for Christmas Day.

"I'll sign off now, boys," Bill reported she had said. "But look out for our bombs under your Christmas tree in Vittel."

Sally's prophecy we could take or leave, but the news of the Bulge was actual. It was very bad, and was heavy in all our minds.

We had a moment's cheer when we went to make up; Chester Stratton had found a hoard of left-over favors from a forgotten gala and had used them to decorate our dressing rooms. Mine had a long and splendid gold trumpet with tassels, a crown of gold to match, and a paper basket of rose petals. Bob had a red striped deck chair a bit too reminiscent of sunny beaches, some tinsel daggers, and also some hearts and a whole bower of paper flowers.

Roger and Erik had a spinning-wheel, and two blond paper wigs in which they looked very nice indeed as they sat at the spinning-wheel and sang "The King of Thule" from Faust.

As we dressed we wished we were playing *Nanook of the North* in furs and parkas, but we did the best we could, and tufts of sweaters and GI underwear protruded from all our Wimpole Street laces and silks. On the stage the curtains gave up trying to be solid Wimpole Street walls, and bellied out with the freezing draft that filled them.

The rest of us could at least move about, but for an hour Kit had to lie in that same draft, bound to her sofa. When I touched her hand it was like ice, and when I had to go off the stage I felt I couldn't bear to leave her there. But when the act was over she only asked Gert to take the quill pens out of the inkstands.

"They're revolving like pin-wheels," she said. "And they make me dizzy."

I had thought perhaps the auditorium would be warmer, but it was no better and our audience was wrapped in blankets and more blankets.

Kit said she had a sudden memory of our other hospital audience in Bagnoli when it was so sweltering that they wore no shirts and at the matinees a chink of light would pick up the glisten of their sweating bodies, and she worried because their casts might be unbearably hot. Now she worried that they might congeal in them.

We finished the play, our breath floating around us like wed-

THE B.O.W.S.

139

ding veils, our words freezing in the air till we thought we might
bump into sentences in the third act left over from the second.

There was a stove in the room where Kit and Brian saw the
men afterwards, and we had hot coffee which gave us courage
to face the sub-zero Villa Berthe, where we huddled into Kit's
room for a few minutes' talk.

Kit was laughing because I had reminded her of the contracts
made with all the theaters she played in America, stating the
exact temperature needed for her comfort.

"I don't know how you stood it tonight, Kit," said Nancy.

"I had to," said Kit matter-of-factly. "And anyway, I had
asked God not to let me be a nuisance by getting sick on the
tour, and I would take care of the rest." She laughed again. "I'll
admit that when I was on the sofa I was sure I would never get
off it—I would just have to stay there, frozen into a permanent
S."

"I thought we would all be frozen when Madame said good
night to us," I said. Madame was the only name by which we
knew the woman who ran the Hôtel les Tilleurs. She was thin
and handsome and indifferent, and she reminded me of a story
I had read in the mysterious and dreadful days of the German
occupation when no news came out of France but rumors and
fiction. This had been a curious fabrication that insisted that the
constant indifference of the French had mutilated the very fiber
of the Germanic soul, and now I thought if anyone could accom-
plish that, Madame was the one to do it.

She did her best with Unit 319. Nancy's quick bright smiles
and Kit's warm one were received with the same uninterest, and
the only acknowledgment was that she allowed an ash to fall
from her perpetual cigarette onto the dirty patience cards spread
as perpetually before her.

She always wore black, of no description and of no kind; it
was simply the ultimate definition of black. At night when we
came from the theater we would find her smoking and dealing
the cards. "*Bon soir*" would come our cheerful voices. Her eyelids would flicker as she examined a card. "*Bon soir*" would come
almost inaudibly from her careful lips.

Yet from our private ice-boxes we would hear her in her

kitchen, and out of our sight she would indulge in shrill harsh screams of laughter.

There were no newspapers in Vittel. We had to depend on rumor or what we gathered from the men who came back-stage, and our own possible emergency was the center of scuttlebutt. "Will we be bombed?" we asked, looking at the brilliant moon that made us vulnerable. "Undoubtedly," we were assured. We had no facts, but we knew that the news of the Bulge was worse, because when we left our mess we passed a large map of the war front, and we watched silently every night as an officer took out the pins that marked our gains and slowly retreated them. The distances looked minute on the big map, but we knew that each pin represented a loss and a price paid for it that we dared not estimate.

Once an airman stood and watched with us. "When I remember the lousy breaks in weather we've had, sometimes I think God is a terrific pro-Nazi," he said. "We only need three good days to stop this Bulge."

In the midst of this Christmas came—the darkest, we thought, we had ever known. Every morning as we heard the planes fly out our thoughts went with them, and we prayed hard for those three good days.

We were to give two performances on Christmas Day, so Nancy arranged that we would have our own party the day before, after we had been to the hospital. It was to be in a restaurant about ten miles away, and General Devers had offered his own chef for the occasion, but if it hadn't all been so thoughtfully planned I think we might have begged off.

We gathered at the hospital about two o'clock on Christmas Eve, and we were relieved to find that we wouldn't have to worry about singing carols, as the hospital had already arranged for them, and we heard the singers as we went into the entrance hall.

All we had to do, then, was go from bed to bed with our *santons*, the Christmas figures Nancy had brought from Marseilles; we each had a bag of them and a general meeting was called when we saw them. *Santons* come in different sizes and these were the smallest, and the meeting passed a resolution to warn the patients that they were not to be mistaken for pills. Then we divided into groups of three and went toward the wards and into the core and heart of Christmas.

In the corridors on stretchers lay men just brought down from the front, cold in the drafts that penetrated from the halls. But they greeted us as if they were safe and warm in the homes they must have been thinking of. In the wards they laughed and smiled and joked with us, and promised not to swallow the *santons*. Some of them said they would send them home as souvenirs, they were just right to put in a letter.

We went from ward to ward and they were all the same, and the sound of the carols wove itself in and out of their laughter, and here and there they sang, too.

There was just one who was quiet and far off, though as we passed he gave us a hesitant smile. The nurse took Kit aside.

"We've just had to tell him that his young wife died having their first baby," she said.

Kit went and sat by him, and put her arms around him. "There's nothing I can say," she told him.

"No, ma'am," he whispered, and patted her arm as if he were trying to comfort her.

We stayed all afternoon in the hospital, and the last man who wished us a Merry Christmas had his leg in a huge cast from which half his foot protruded. He had tied a bow of ribbon on his big toe, and hung it with tinsel and Christmas bells.

"It's just a simple little tree," he said, "but it's the best I could do this year."

As we went down to wait for our transportation, and pick up my Bob, I remembered Nancy's carol. "God rest ye merry, gentlemen," I said to myself. "Let nothing ye dismay."

We waited for the cars in a room hung with small caps and coats and mufflers. Bob said there was a party in the hospital for the children of Vittel; the soldiers had made decorations for a tree, and toys and rag dolls, and everybody in the hospital had contributed candy rations.

We heard a great chattering outside and then the door opened and the children came in. This had been the first party some of them had known, and the baby mouths showed traces of the first chocolate they had ever eaten. One mite had still two pieces in her hand, and put one in her mouth and chewed it as if trying to solve a mystery. Then she quickly popped in the other piece. "Please forgive me," she said, "but I am all at once greedy about chocolate."

They had been singing French carols under the tree, we gathered from their excited exclamations, and there must have been a play or a charade for some of the chocolate smears were flanked by bright uneven amateur rouge circles.

Their parents urged them into coats that were mostly made of patches of fur stitched together, and when they were on they looked like the rabbits from which the fur had come. The clothes under the coats had been everything from preserved finery to threadbare remnants, but the children's faces were all the same round spangles of delight.

As we drove the ten miles to the restaurant I found myself still wondering if we should have attempted a party. Christmas dinner in a restaurant has always seemed a dreary thing to me. Christmas dinner has always meant a family and old friends and firelight and games afterwards, in which everyone had to join.

But when we drew up at la Bonne Auberge it was a small white building with the look of a New England farmhouse, homelike and hospitable, and some of my private doubts subsided. And when we went inside they vanished. Erik Martin and Keinert Wolff had given up the hospital visit and had gone out early and made our dining room into a Christmas welcome. There were great clusters of mistletoe on the table and the mantelpiece, and they had set up a tree and somehow found ornaments to shine on it. The kitchen, where General Devers' chef was in charge, was off the room, and its busy sounds and warm smell had a coziness of its own. It was going to be a lovely party.

The dinner was wonderful, and made me feel sorry for the people at home. We drank a combined toast to General Devers and his chef and the chestnut soup, and the turkey which looked very Roman with its head still on, and the salad with cream dressing, and the amazing *tarte* at the end.

Kit and Brian had provided the dinner, and George Keane had presented us with champagne, and we had brought presents for

each other and Keinert Wolff had written jingles for everyone.
We especially cheered the one dedicated to Emily Lawrence.

> From bed to bed in every camp
> Walks the Lady with the Lamp
> But not so pale—no figure frail
> Has the Barretts' Emily Nightingale.

This inspired Kit to make a speech of admiration to Kay, and
she thanked him for all the work he had done in the hospitals,
and Brian raised his glass and said: "To Emily and Kay and the
Battle of the Nightingales."

I looked across the table at Nancy and thought how right she
had been. It would have been terrible not to have been together
like this. As long as people can be, they should be, I thought
rather confusedly. We all felt the same way, and deluged her
with congratulations. And I rose with a toast to her myself.

"To Nancy *Santon* Claus!" I said, in a pun that I remember
now with a deep blush.

There was another party in la Bonne Auberge; they were
French and Russians and their singing came to us from the next
room. We sang, too, all the carols we had rehearsed in Dijon,
and if the results were not harmonious, this time the Barretts
were.

We had a last toast to each other and everyone we loved, and
then the singing from the next room enticed us, and like any
neighbors at Christmas we went to call. They couldn't all speak
our language and we couldn't speak theirs, but it didn't matter—
it was Christmas, and what we said had the same meaning.

Christmas Day passed with the two performances and we re-
sumed our usual routine. We visited Carmel White at the Red
Cross at Bains-les-Bains, and Kit went to Domremy to see where
Joan of Arc had been born.

Bob was much better but still at the hospital. As he was a patient he was never told the password for the day which we had
to use when we went to our mess, but we told him when the
day was over.

One day it had been Trouble. "That's odd," said Bob; "of
course I know it has no connection, but they told me just before

I came over that the hospital has been alerted to evacuate in twenty-four hours."

We looked at each other. "Maybe it's a good thing we are assimilated captains, after all," said Emily.

Bob went back to his ward when his part was finished, and after the play I left a note for him at the hospital on my way to the doubtful refuge of the Hôtel les Tilleurs. I had been moved there, from the Villa Berthe, to a smaller room.

Madame was at her usual place, at her usual game of patience.

There was a field telephone in her parlor, and this night there was an officer waiting beside it.

"I guess we get the raid tonight," he said when he saw me. "They told me to stand by for the warning."

I asked if there was a shelter and he said there was a nice ditch across the street. I smiled, and he began to pace the short length of the room.

I looked at Madame but she was as impassive as if she were deaf. She turned a red card and put it on a black.

"*Bon soir, madame,*" I said.

"*Bon soir,*" she said, and the ash from the cigarette in her mouth fell with the word.

I went up the stairs and looked back from the top. The officer was pacing, up and down, up and down. The figure at the table might have been an automaton.

Dear Madame, I thought, you play your cards so surely; almost as if you know which way they will fall.

Upstairs Emily was waiting for me, standing in the door of her room braiding her hair for the night. Brian joined us. "I hear the paratroopers have been pouring down like hail," he said; "they're supposed to have dropped about four hundred." I told him the officer expected a raid. Brian asked if we were nervous, and we said no as convincingly as we could. He told us to keep our flashlights handy and our clothes ready to get into quickly, and if we felt squeamish to call him.

Just then all the lights went out, and we waited, but nothing happened. "Well, good night," said Brian in the dark, and we said, "Good night," and closed our doors.

I got into bed and listened to regular footsteps on the icy road outside. That was the sentry, I knew. Planes went over and I recognized them for our own. What might come I had no idea, or how I would behave. There seemed to be very little use in being frightened for myself; it was all too big for any personal emotion to matter. I would just try to take it as it came, I thought, as finally I went to sleep. But a long time afterwards Bob showed me the note I had sent after him to the hospital.

Bob: If we are taken prisoners by the Germans and you get out first, please do not try to find me, but go right to Beekman Place and wait for me there. MARGALO.

CHAPTER FIFTEEN

VITTEL was never bombed. There was a raid that night, as they had expected, but a village eight miles away got it. Next morning George Keane told us we would leave for Paris as planned, and we couldn't help feeling relieved, but we didn't know then that Vittel would escape the Bulge, and we felt guilty, too, at being free to go.

We thought of the hospital and la Bonne Auberge and the children at the party and we wished they were like Nancy's *santons*, and we could put them in with our helmets and gas masks and take them to safety.

We touched Dijon again on the way to Paris, with just enough time between trains for a glimpse of General Larkin and Ed Comm, and one short toast to the New Year. We raised our glasses and said, "To home!" and we meant it for all the men who had answered so simply, "Why, to get home," when we asked them what they were fighting for.

It was snowing when we approached Paris, and Kit stood in the train corridor trying to rub enough of the frosted window clear to peer through. It was very early in the morning and we could barely see the châteaux in their parks as we passed them.

All through our tour I had been hoping for this moment, and now that it had come I was like a child who rushes eagerly to a party and then hesitates on the doorstep, suddenly shy. I had wanted so much to see Paris again, to see what had happened to her, and what she was like in her new liberty, but now I was almost afraid.

The train snuffled into the station, choked a few times, and stopped. Brian and the other men tugged the windows open, ready to hand out the bags. The air came in, foggy and wet and unfamiliar.

I missed something. "Is this the right station?" I asked Brenda.

"Of course, darling," she said.

But it didn't sound like a French station, and then I realized there was no sound at all. No screams, no threats, no entreaties, no hysteria.

"No porters," I said, accounting for the calm. But someone was taking the bags as they were pushed out. "Hello, Margalo," said a voice I knew and I made up for the lack of porters and contributed a few screams of my own. It was Josh Logan, one of the best directors the theater ever lost to the Army. We were overjoyed to see him, and he said he had a date for us that evening, a surprise.

We were going to the Crillon, a hotel I had only sighed at when I had been in Paris before. It was Army-requisitioned now, and I wondered about the modest roof that had sheltered me in 1935. I asked our driver if it was requisitioned, too. "Yes, ma'am," he said, "they put the jeep drivers there."

I looked out of the car at this new Paris. We passed Maxim's, and I saw it was now the Maple Leaf Club for Servicemen. Everywhere there were British and American signs and clubs, and the traffic was steady and controlled and I missed absurdly the headlong fits and starts and the near collisions and the Gershwin toots of the French taxis.

The Crillon waited for us, indifferent to the scars of machine gun bullets on its dignified façade. Inside it might have been still 1935 so far as the clerks behind the desk went. They wore the same impeccable white vests and tail coats, and their manners were urbane and beautiful as they assigned us to rooms that were luxurious to look at and freezing to live in, since the Army's coal supply was exhausted. On our way we passed two men and I heard them say that there was perpetual snow in their rooms. When I got to mine I wondered why it wasn't ice.

"Talking about it won't help," said Emily Lawrence and filled her tub with cold water and sat in it.

"Emily, Emily!" Brian remonstrated when he heard about it. "How could you do such a thing! It's too cold even to take your clothes off."

Emily said she had wanted to get her circulation going.

"Did you?" asked Brian.

"Not altogether," said Emily, "but it made the room seem warmer afterwards."

Josh's surprise for us that night was the *Folies-Bergère*. "I thought it would be a good old-fashioned first-night-in-Paris thing to do," he said, and we thought so, too.

Whatever else had changed, the Folies was the same. The only difference was the GI audience and the temperature of the theater. But the chorus was as Spartan as Emily, and we sat with our coats on and gazed at it open-mouthed. Not because it was naked, but because it seemed to be able to stand it.

Though as we walked home together, Chester Stratton sighed. "Gosh," he said thoughtfully, "I'd almost forgotten about nudes."

We opened the next night at Versailles. I had been there as a sight-seer but I never dreamed that I would walk on the stage of the old theater, with its boxes that were so low and near us that the heads of their occupants were on the level of our carpet and bobbed about like decapitations left over from the French Revolution.

I shared Kit's dressing room and her stove, and we would get there early and sit making up while Nancy read aloud to us. Kit loves being read to; she has a passion for old-fashioned sentiment, and Nancy hunted everywhere we went for new and choice examples, one of the most successful having been an epic called *Nancy No Good*, about a little girl who had had a peculiarly tough time at boarding school.

I had done a little hunting myself, and I had found a Tauchnitz edition of *Little Men*, and Nancy began it at Versailles. Louisa Alcott was an integral part of our childhood, and Kit's first engagement in London had been as Jo in *Little Women*, and we prepared for an orgy of nostalgia. Nancy reads beautifully, and her ear for accent is perfect, and Professor Bhaer became very lifelike as she gave soft gutturals to his speeches.

Kit listened for a while and then she stopped Nancy.

"It's no good," she said. "I can't stand the German accent. Can't you give him a French one? In London they made him French."

"I'll read him straight," said Nancy, "but listen to this."

"When I was a little lad I used to tell lies; ach! what fibs they were, and my old Grandmother cured me of it—how do you think? . . . The dear old Grandmother said, 'I shall help you to remember.' With that she drew out my tongue and snipped the end with her scissors till the blood ran."

Kit looked at us in horror.

Nancy put the book down. "I could read him in any accent you suggest, Kit," she said. "But if he has any more tender tales like that he'll still come out German."

Though we were playing at Versailles we stayed at the Crillon, going back and forth by bus, which meant an early dinner and getting back after the dining room was closed, so we reverted to old habits and saved our dinner rolls and left them in the rack behind the desk with our keys, retrieving them when we came in, the clerks handing them to us as formally as if they had been diplomatic papers filed for safe-keeping.

The dining room had kept the same outward elegance as the rest of the hotel, and deferential waiters served us with all the old ritual, though the food was Army and the flourish of a silver cover only revealed the familiarity of Vienna sausage and spaghetti. We would have liked to encourage them with a pretense of grandeur on our own part and brightened the tables with something more colorful than our Special Service uniforms, but an evening came when Betty Brewer made up for all our drabness.

Bob Hester had got leave, and permission to come to Paris in his own plane. It was snowing hard when he telephoned her from Foggia.

"I asked him if it was safe to fly," she told us, "and he was quite scornful!"

We were all at dinner when they came together to the dining room entrance, and the maître d'hôtel went to meet them with that special unhurried rush that denotes the appearance of important guests. He bowed and brought them to a table, walking proudly. "But, look," he seemed to say, "this is like old times."

Betty had piled her hair high on her head, and she had defied the cold with a thin, brilliantly red silk dress. She was the gayest thing the Crillon had seen in many a long day, and she sat touching the earrings she wore and flirting outrageously with her bridegroom, while we all watched shamelessly and waiters hovered like doves.

Before we finished in Versailles Kit had a brief meeting with General Eisenhower, at his headquarters. She had an appointment, but just as the time approached, Kit said, there was a sudden outbreak of jumping to attention and saluting, and General Bradley and his staff appeared from nowhere and swept on into the inner office.

She waited, she said, and the hour got nearer the matinee, and she began to worry about etiquette. You just didn't walk out on the Supreme Head of the Allied Forces, and yet you didn't hold the curtain, either. She was torn between her duty as an assimilated captain and her duty as an actress and her overwhelming desire to meet the General in her own person, and she was beginning to be a little dizzy when Ike himself came out and said, "Hi, come on in."

There wasn't time to talk very long, but Kit said she had to think faster than she ever had in her life when he asked her why the Barretts was a success with the GIs.

"But it all clarified for me," said Kit, "and I told him it was very simple. It was just a perfectly plain story with a hero and heroine and an ogre, and it had love and excitement and suspense." She looked at us with an amazed relief. "I couldn't have put it like that before—it just came to me. But you know," she said, "the General said he hadn't been sure himself that it would be a success!"

From Versailles we went to Sacha Guitry's theater in Paris, vacant because M. Guitry was imprisoned as a collaborationist, though it still had the staff that had worked with him for twenty-three years.

"What did he do?" Nancy asked them. They shrugged evasively.

"Oh, he was naughty."

"How naughty?" Nancy persisted.

"Oh," they said, "he had a little bust of Hitler in the lobby and he made speeches explaining we must be kind to the Germans."

The theater was run just as it had been before M. Guitry began to be naughty. The stagehands all wore berets and his old wardrobe mistress lived there in a room in which she kept five dogs. While we were there a good many of the sandwiches provided for us by the Red Cross disappeared into that room, and we heard the joyful barks that met them. The dogs drank coffee, too, it appeared. But how she fed them when we weren't there was a mystery in a city that couldn't feed itself. I used to wonder about every dog I saw, especially the chic poodles. I was tempted to run after their owners and ask how they did it, and how they could afford to have them so beautifully clipped.

Kit had Sacha Guitry's suite at the theater. A greenroom, not large but most comfortably furnished, and a dressing room that was a perfect example of the phrase "all done with mirrors." Mirrors concealed the washstand, and mirrors concealed the door that led to the dressing room of his leading lady, and we were sure mirrors would conceal what the English advertisements refer to so delicately as the usual offices, but they were either nonexistent or too well concealed, because we never found them.

The greenroom was useful for visitors, and one night Kit called me in to meet Gertrude Stein and Alice Toklas there. When they heard I knew Carl Van Vechten they asked me to tea the next day, as they had a book I could take to him.

There was a matinee that day, and not much time between performances, so Kit lent me her car, and I kept my make-up on, which gave me an extra half hour or so.

Bob came with me, and we drove to the rue Christophe. The concierge looked like one of the less attractive characters from *The Two Orphans*, and when we asked for Miss Stein she jerked a bitten thumb upwards and held up two fingers. We walked up the two flights to Miss Stein's apartment and rang the bell.

A maid answered it, took a startled look at me, and shut the door again.

"Maybe I shouldn't have left my make-up on," I said to Bob.

"Maybe we shouldn't have come," said Bob.

I began to feel self-conscious, and dabbed at my face with my handkerchief. "Shall we try again or just go?" said Bob, when the door opened and Miss Stein herself looked out at us curiously.

"What do you want?" she asked.

We explained timidly that she had asked us to tea.

"Oh, did I?" she said. "Well, come on in, then."

We must have looked uncertain, because she galvanized us into movement by giving us each a boyish push that landed us over the threshold, into her famous living room where every available space was filled with the paintings of Picasso.

Her publisher was there, and she sat beside him and went on with the conversation we had interrupted.

Bob studied the paintings, and I sat feeling completely inadequate to the situation, until Miss Stein's white poodle Basket took pity on me and made a few gentle passes which were comforting.

Then Miss Stein leapt abruptly from her sofa and came over to me. "What's your name?" she said, and I told her.

"What's his?" pointing to Bob.

She sat beside me. She had on a long, heavy tweed skirt that gave the impression that even when Gertrude Stein was not in it it possessed a quiet, rugged life of its own; she had on a bright red sweater and an assortment of scarves, one of which looked remarkably like a serviette. She talked with the words and manner of a New England farmer and every now and then she would scratch her close-cropped white head.

I was aware of her age when she was not looking at me, but when she was I forgot it in the brilliance and vitality of her gaze, which was so direct and so penetratingly focused that it was impossible to be conscious of anything else.

I asked her about Picasso's portrait of her which hung over the fireplace, and she said she had posed for it eighty times.

"That takes a lot of patience."

"But I have a lot of patience."

"Is it cultivated or natural?"

"No, it's not cultivated," she said. "It's because I don't like to make a fuss; if people ask me to do things, I do them." She paused. "That seems an odd thing to come from one who has headed the modern art movement."

Alice Toklas came in with a large tray of tea things; she also wore a long tweed skirt, and a red bandanna on her head, tied to show a small black fringe of hair.

"Ross, will you help Miss Toklas to pass the tea?" said Miss Stein to Bob.

"No, lovey, I can do it myself," said Alice.

"But I don't want you to, Pussy," said Gertrude.

During tea she told us that the Germans had occupied her apartment, but had taken nothing, and that she and Alice and Basket had ridden eighteen hours in a taxi to get to Paris when the Germans left.

I asked her if she owned her house in the country.

"No," she said, and chose a New England word again. "It was hired. I wouldn't own a house; if you own something you spend too much time trying to get away from it."

As we drove back in the twilight I found myself vaguely humming. "What *is* that?" I said to Bob; "I can't remember."

"It's 'The Owl and the Pussy Cat,'" he said, and sang the words: "The Owl and the Pussy Cat went to sea in a beautiful pea-green boat."

"Oh, yes," I said and sang along with him. "With lots of money and plenty of honey wrapped up in a five pound note."

The city was lovely in the dusk. Up the narrow street we drove to the theater. In only a few hours it would be curfew, and we would walk home through the dark streets. There was still gaiety to be found, if we cared enough, or had money enough; there were restaurants where you could get a black market dinner for two for about fifty dollars, and there were night clubs that we could grope our way to. Mostly the British and Americans patronized them, and rarely a few French people, but not the French that we saw walking in the streets in the daytime hours or met in apartments that had been stripped by the Germans.

For themselves the B.O.W.S. did very little. We were leading separate lives again, we each had friends in Paris, and a great many, and we were always running into more.

I saw Janet Flanner there, and I remember how carefully she collected the cigarette stubs after lunch. "Four stubs make a cigarette, you know," she said, though I hadn't known.

We talked about Paris and its difference. "And yet," I said, "it's still full of Americans." We laughed. "Remember the Ritz?" I said, "with the bar always jammed with everybody you knew from America, and the tea garden outside and the beautiful clothes and the Chicago voices, and never a sign of a French person? And the shops and the dressmakers and the low franc and the lovely things to buy with it."

"Now you are in Paris and can't buy anything," said Janet, "and the Americans are here because they have work to do."

Kit had told me how she had always felt ill at ease in Paris in the old days. "Everyone was so smart," she said, "and so busy about clothes, and they went so many places and did so many things, and I used to feel awkward and I couldn't fit in. I never seemed to have anything to contribute."

She liked this new sober Paris better, and perhaps I did too, though I never got used to the eeriness that came with curfew.

I had known the lights and sounds of Paris, and loved them, but now at night there was nothing. We walked in the dark, the snow brushing its wings against our faces, and some of my childhood terror of the dark would come back to me. The buildings seemed to shrink to share it, and the churches grow taller above them. We would stop sometimes, thinking we had heard a sound behind us, and time seemed to stop with us. It might have been the medieval wolf packs or the Germans of yesterday at our heels, and we waited, listening, but it was only the sound of our own footsteps that had startled us, and we would walk on, feeling we were the only people in the world.

It was time for us to leave. General Solbert had wanted Kit to stay in Paris till the end of her scheduled time overseas, but she asked to be sent on, nearer the front. Like Rome and Marseilles, Paris had no real need of us, and we could be more useful where there was no other entertainment. "As near the front as possible," she said, and she was delighted when George Keane told us we were going to Holland. "Will we be close to the front?" she asked again, and George said we certainly would be; about twenty miles from it in Maastricht and about eight in Heerlen.

"You will all have to sign papers again on secrecy," he told us, "and you must wear your helmets at all times as there are plenty of buzz bombs where we are going."

We had them on when we left the Crillon. Bob Hester stood and watched us out of sight, and Betty looked after him, long after the bus had turned a corner, and he was gone. Then she curled up in a ball and hid her face. If she saw him again, it would be when the war was over.

When we got to the station it was as though we had left Paris already. Arc lamps made triangular pools of light and soldiers headed for the front, passed through them, their faces immobile in the light.

Our old feeling of being where we belonged came flooding back, and our old feeling of being a unit. We had had another interlude and it had been pleasant, but this was better.

"Sixteen," said George Keane as he counted us on to the train. Our departure had been orderly this time but he sighed with relief from habit.

He gave us his usual titbit of news which he always kept for the last minute.

"You're supposed to arrive in Brussels at 0700 hours, but the train is always six to seven hours late, and there's no diner." He handed us each a carton of K rations. "You can use this for breakfast if we're late."

Army time confuses me and I said so. "0700 hours sounds late enough; I don't see how we could be later."

"0700 hours is seven o'clock in the morning," said Elaine Perry, who always knew things like that down to the last split second.

We prepared for a long trip and K rations for breakfast, but French trains can't be depended on and we arrived at 0600 hours, a whole hour ahead of time. "That's six o'clock," Elaine informed me as we got off, but she didn't need to; I know six o'clock in the morning just by the way I feel.

There was a little coffee shop in the station with a counter that suggested food. There was a long table down the center of the room and we all dropped wearily into chairs. Brian looked up and down the table. "My God," he said. "Don't our women look awful!"

"Awful," agreed the rest of the men.

In the precipitation of our arrival none of us had time for powder or lipstick, or even to wash, and we were wearing the small khaki-colored knitted caps with vizors that the Army issues to be worn under helmets. They are not becoming at the best of times, and now we looked like a faded picture of an 1890 ball team. Betty and Elaine wore their steel helmets as well, and they had settled well down over their ears, and their hair straggled in uncombed tangles over their shoulders.

"My pal there," said Chester Stratton, pointing to me, "used to be nice looking. Now look at her." Everybody looked at me. I was wearing two pairs of GI drawers, two pairs of wool stockings, slacks, a sweater of my own, a GI sweater over that, and a German airman's fleece-lined coat.

"She looks awful," the men chorused.

"When I think how they looked when we left New York," sighed Brian.

I said that I didn't care how I looked; I was cold.

"Talking about it won't make you warmer," repeated Emily.

"Emily," I said, "you talk like a hand-painted motto."

"I think," said Kit, "we would all feel better if we had some hot coffee."

We had coffee, ersatz but hot, and started for Maastricht. It was a long drive and we stopped constantly to wait while convoys of British and Americans passed us on their way to the front in trucks and tanks and loaded onto anti-aircraft guns.

Troops almost always had waved and shouted to us when they passed us, but none of these did. They looked back at us, expressionless, unseeing, as if they had drawn apathy around them in protection; and they were silent among themselves, as if they were gathered together in something that needed no more words.

We drove on and into the sound of guns. The anti-aircraft guns were firing in the square when we got to the Red Cross center in Maastricht, where we waited to be billeted.

George Keane came to tell us that most of us would be with civilians and to give us an unexpected briefing. "The Red Cross found a definite local indifference to you as actors," he told us, "but when motion pictures were mentioned there was a rush to billet you; so remember—you are *all* film stars."

Elaine, Betty, and Emily were with the local doctor; Bob and I with the banker, and McKay Morris drew the dentist. Our billet was charming and our hostess' name was Mevrouw Drogleever Fortwyn van Ryckevorsel, and after much practice we were able to pronounce half of it. Luckily for us she spoke delightful English but Dutch sounded incomprehensible, and we wondered what Bill Noon would do with it.

General Simpson asked us to dinner at his headquarters our first night there and made us feel wonderfully at home. His staff dined with us, and it might have been an occasion of formality but it was as simple and unelaborate as a dinner with old friends, and if it hadn't been for an occasional buzz bomb we might have been in Vermont.

A low blast came during dinner, and the General raised an eyebrow. "They must be way off their target," he said.

Gert asked how far away that one had been and the General said about three miles. "Really?" we murmured, giving a passable imitation of mere casual interest. Another exploded almost at once, and the Barretts' assumption of indifference was possibly the finest performance they had ever given.

Whether it was for that one or for our others, we were never sure, but after dinner the General presented us with the patch of the Ninth Army, for which we were to play.

Our theater was two flights up in an old building that harbored a dance hall on the ground floor. The dance hall functioned at the same time we did and furnished incidental music at unexpected moments. The band was fond of the good old tunes, and when "Yes, Sir, That's my Baby" came in the middle of one of her scenes Kit said she had an almost uncontrollable desire to acknowledge it with a brief Charleston.

The performance was to begin at seven, but when we got to the theater we found it had been filled since four in the afternoon. The men had come with magazines and books and K rations, and they did that all the time we were there.

When they came back-stage we found it hard to realize that these were the men who were preparing to push into Germany.

They were splendidly casual, and one of them took us rather severely to task for the bust that was part of our stage setting. It rested on the mantelpiece to illustrate Brian's speech to Kit: "I have seen this room more times than I can remember . . . and that bust of Homer is an old friend."

"Don't you know that isn't Homer?" said our critic. "That's Voltaire."

We explained to him that Homer had been a casualty of travel and that Bill Noon had used the only substitute he could find, feeling that if a Yorkshire terrier could play a spaniel, it was all right for Voltaire to pinch-hit for Homer.

The performance had gone smoothly and Bill Noon had had no trouble with his two or three Maastricht helpers.

"What did he do?" I asked Bob. "He couldn't put an O on a Dutch word—there wouldn't be room."

But Bob told me that inexplicably, Mr. Noon, Irish for generations, spoke fluent and authentic Dutch.

The town of Maastricht was pleasant, and Bob and I would walk about it, very proud of the Ninth Army patch on our sleeves, but self-conscious about our good steel helmets. None of the citizens or children had them, though the anti-aircraft guns were alert in the square. In one or two of the shop windows were signs in English: "This shop was German friendly." The Dutch put them there, our hosts told us, for the benefit of the Allies, so that they might avoid them if they wished, but, they added proudly, there were only a very few of them, and the whole of the country had averaged only five per cent collaborationist.

On one of our walks a young man leaned from a window and called to us, "Please, aktor, aktrice, please come in my house."

"It's McKay's dentist," said Bob, and we went in.

We had heard from McKay that his life with the dentist was a colorful one. The three children in the house were volcanoes of energy, they shouted in play, and the dentist's patients shouted in pain, and the dentist's brother, who was a concert pianist, practiced unperturbed through both, and when none of this was happening, which was very seldom, a Polish officer guest seized the opportunity to raise his voice in songs of his homeland.

The three children were at lunch when we went in, food keeping them momentarily quiet, and we were introduced to Mrs. Dentist, who wore slacks and was very attractive.

The rooms were hung with enormous oil paintings, to which the dentist gestured as he gave us chairs.

"A few things of mine," he said, dismissing them. He brought us a book and asked us, please, to sign our names and American addresses, as, please, it was very important. We did, and he leaned towards us with fervor.

"I have written a little play," he said. Then he relaxed and smiled winningly at us. "Please, I will now explain the plot." He leaned back in his chair, and put his fingertips together. "It is based," he said, "on the political structure of ancient Greece as compared to the modern world. Do you like it?"

Bob said it was quite an angle.

"It is fantastically exciting; I will describe it to you."

But we said we would have to come again—we were on our way to lunch. We would have to hurry or the mess would be closed, we added for good measure.

"Then I will send it to you," he said.

"Thank you," said Bob, sounding a shade too grateful, and we rose.

"But wait," said the dentist, "I want you to hear some discs of music I have made to go with the play. It will hardly take an hour."

But we said again that, alas, the mess would be closing in only a few minutes, and he bowed, and we shook hands formally all round.

As we walked away from the house he leaned from the window again. "Tell Mr. Morris," he shouted, "I do not understand why he is never home."

On our last night in Maastricht Bob and I had supper with our own host and hostess. Food is such a tragic problem to civilians that we hated to eat even a mouthful that belonged to them, but they urged us so sincerely that we accepted.

They were waiting for us after the play in their living room that had so many charming things in it. Mellow furniture, soft blue delft, and a delicate Chinese figure on the mantelpiece that they had brought from the Dutch East Indies where they had once lived.

The judge of Maastricht was with them, and they had a sparkle of excitement about them as if this was not just a small party but an event. They told us about the supper they had managed for us with the greatest delight. The judge, our hostess' brother, had bicycled eight miles to get some milk! There were fresh mushrooms and mashed potatoes, fruit salad, and a bottle of a very special wine. The mushrooms, they explained, were from the famous Maastricht Caves. We told them we had seen the Caves only that morning.

"You have seen them?" said our host. "Did you see the pictures?"

When the Germans were in Holland they had stripped the museums of their treasures of paintings and stored them for safety in the Caves, sublimely confident that they were preserving them for Germany. Now the Germans were gone but the paintings were still in Holland.

I had gone to the Caves thinking of damp and darkness and stalactites and unpleasant animal life. But the Maastricht Caves were something I could never have imagined. They were clean and white and well lit and air-conditioned, and contained sleeping quarters and a hospital. They ran for sixteen miles in an intricate maze in which it seemed impossible not to get lost. But the Dutch knew it by heart, and no one knows how many British and American paratroopers and airmen owe their lives to these underground passages where the Dutch hid them till they could escape through them to Belgium.

The paintings were stored in a small room behind three heavily barred doors. We signed a register before the guard took us through them, closing each one carefully after us. Inside there was all the art of Holland—Rembrandts, Rubens, Franz Hals, Van Dycks, and Vermeers. They were hung on frames as material is in a decorator's shop and there were so many that we stood pressed against the wall as the guard turned them for us to see. And in a separate niche he showed us a rolled canvas that was Rembrandt's *Night Watch.*

"You have seen it," said our host when we told him. "It is good to know it is safe. But we Dutch miss our beautiful things. If we could only see them ourselves it would give us heart, but we are not allowed to; civilians are not allowed in the Caves." He paused. "But I am glad you have seen them; when they are seen they live again for a little while."

We talked till very late. The carillon from the cathedral peeled out the hours in its chimes and we heard the spaced explosions of distant buzz bombs. I remembered how eagerly our hostess had met us the day we were billeted, how she had given us tea and talked with rushes of words. This night it was the same; they talked as though their words had been stemmed too long, and at the end they brought out an album of pictures of their plantation in Java and they showed them to us as if it had been a life on another planet.

In the morning the children were sledding around the anti-aircraft guns as we wrapped ourselves into our cars. We were all in when McKay's dentist came hurrying up. "Good-bye, aktors, aktrices," he said, and cast four manuscripts through the window onto McKay's reluctant lap.

As we started Kay gave a hunted look back at his late host. "Margalo," he said. "I'm *tired*."

CHAPTER SIXTEEN

"How FAR is Heerlen from Germany?" I asked Bob as we came near to it.

"About as far as First Avenue from Beekman Place," he said, to make it clear for me.

It was a tired, drab little town, eight miles from the front just as George Keane had said. The hotel lobby was filled with medics just in from the field, and they stared at me as I went with Bob to register. The sergeant behind the desk stared too, and as he handed me my key he gave me a warning.

"You're the only woman in the hotel and there's no catch on the toilet door, so look out."

I promised him earnestly that I would, but he only looked at me severely as if he was wondering what the Army was coming to.

The other women were all together at another hotel, and I hoped they could be less wary.

We had just time to get some lunch and go straight to where we were to play at two o'clock. It was hardly a theater; it was half moving-picture house, half hall. There was a sort of courtyard in back, with an entrance to the stage and an entrance to the theater, and we stood there to watch the men arrive. They came in trucks as they had in Montecatini, but this was no three or four days' rest for them; this was three hours'. They had been literally pulled out of frozen foxholes and loaded on the trucks and when the play was over they would be taken straight back. We tried to imagine what it would be like to be yanked out of a foxhole, put down in front of *The Barretts of Wimpole Street*, and yanked back to a foxhole. We could imagine a dazed GI saying to himself afterwards, "What was that?"

But it would give them three hours out of the cold and the range of the guns, and if they only took it as a chance to go to sleep we would be glad they could. But as they jumped from the trucks they were alert and alive. They had none of the weary numbness of the men at Montecatini; they were so fresh from battle that they still had the keyed intensity of action, and they hailed us good-naturedly as they clattered into the theater, their battle jackets buttoned close, their guns in their hands.

Kit watched them till the last minute before she had to get ready. Just as she turned to go a soldier ran past her, then stopped and looked back and waved to a uniform he thought he knew.

"Hi, nurse," he called. "This is where the poor GI gets culture."

We listened as George Keane went before the curtain to remind them to fasten the safety catches on their weapons.

"At the last show here the men forgot it, and three guns were discharged," he explained. There was a laugh, and then all the catches clicked together like a round of machine-gun fire.

We had the feeling that we were playing to old friends, that day, and back-stage was full of visitors who had adopted us in the same capacity, and stayed on through the performance, wanting to talk more than anything else.

Brian's room was a magnet for callers. Captain Duncan of the Dandy Grays, Baltimore, ambled in to say that he had brought his men in to see the show, but he would like to stick around and talk if nobody minded.

On his heels came a soldier looking for McKay Morris. "They've just pulled me out of a foxhole," he said, "and I want to say hello to Pop." He slid four hand grenades from inside his tunic and laid them on Brian's make-up shelf. "Mind if I leave these here for a while?" he asked. "They get a bit heavy."

Captain Duncan had introduced himself to Gert and discovered that she was a dog-lover. "You'll have to see Killer," he said. "He's my mascot. He's got a bit of shell shock right now, but as soon as he's had some sleep he'll be all right."

Killer sounded like a bloodhound to Gert, and a shell-shocked bloodhound was probably the last thing she wanted to meet but she said it would be lovely.

"I'll send one of my men for him," said Captain Duncan; "I want him to meet the cast."

"Fine," said Gert, "we'll be waiting for him."

We didn't have to wait long. In a few minutes a soldier came in carrying a steel helmet. Killer was sitting inside it, a little black and white Chihuahua.

"He sleeps in my helmet," explained the captain.

"Among other functions," said the soldier.

Gert asked how he had been shell shocked and the captain said they had a bit of a push and he had Killer buttoned in his battle jacket, and the artillery was rather heavy.

"What do you feed him?" asked Gert, who was now getting anxious about Killer's welfare. The captain said, "Spam, C rations, anything. He shared my plum pudding at Christmas and he loved it. He's got the constitution of a lion."

Killer looked anything but a lion as he sat in the helmet, but the captain knew him better than we did, we supposed, and we could only hope he was right.

After the play the men came back as anxious to talk as Captain Duncan had been. Except for an overacceleration there was no sign that they were conscious of what they had come from or what they were going back to. There was a rumor that the Bulge was about to be liquidated and they were on the verge of advancing. "It's not so tough," they said cheerfully; "we're firing into Germany and we don't have to worry about what we hit. We just lay everything flat." The trucks were waiting for them and they had to go, but they gave us a reassurance as they left. "You'll probably hear the mail tonight, but don't worry. It's all outgoing—nothing coming in."

The mail was the bombardment that started at ten that night. It superseded any conception of sound that could be imagined. It rolled in a gigantic never-ceasing thunderous reverberation that shook every stone of every building, and chattered the panes of the windows in terror at the force of this declaration of power. Vr—rroom! it went, vr—rroooom! and the earth shuddered at its announcement of vengeance. Shell after shell pounded into the night with no second's pause between. It began and went on, and in the morning it stopped, and when it did it left not quiet, but a vacuum.

It came every night while we were there, and after the first night we drove over the border into Germany where the Siegfried Line bared its teeth at the destruction of Aachen. The city was gone. The remains of a cathedral writhed against the sky, and that was all.

When we got back to the hotel it seemed hardly possible that food was still being served, that there were people and voices. At mess an officer asked me where we had been. I told him Aachen. "It teaches you not to count your teaspoons and doilies, doesn't it?" he said.

The bombardment had always stopped at eleven in the morning, as punctual as any other mail, but the last morning we were in Heerlen it stopped at seven-thirty and at breakfast they told us why. The last tip of the Bulge had been stopped and the troops were advancing. We could hardly believe that the news we had so longed for had come at last. We had not dared to believe the rumors we had heard when we had first arrived, though we had seen things that made us wonder. Guns had made way for troops on the roads, and that meant advances—we had learned that. And through the performances officers had come in during the intermissions to order men out from even that short respite. "Men of Company X report immediately to your commanding officers." The sound of feet going up the aisles in obedience to emergency was as familiar to us as the catches on the guns clicking to safety. It all added up, and the Bulge was stopped.

We hadn't wanted to leave Heerlen. It was the same as before; we wanted to stay with these men as long as they would have us. We had felt our time with them was too short, but now no extension would have mattered. They were leaving us, as we were leaving them, and where they were going we couldn't follow.

We played a last time to them, wanting the play never to finish, and when they came to say good-bye we wanted never to let them go. They brought us presents. Oranges they had saved from Christmas, and a gallon jar of peaches that one of them had got in Germany, which he presented to McKay.

We went out and stood in the courtyard as the trucks were starting.

"We'll miss you," they called to Kit.

"But what will we do without *you?*" she called to them over the noise of the starting engines.

The trucks lumbered them away and we went into the theater to pack, and in a few hours we were speeding over icy roads to Reims and our last engagement overseas. It was as unreal to us that we were ending as it had been that we would ever begin. It had been coming nearer and nearer, but we had evaded thinking about it. All that we had seen and done had become so much a part of our life that we couldn't imagine any other. Something might still happen, we thought, and we wouldn't have to finish.

But plans for our departure were going steadily ahead; we were once more waiting to be alerted, and there was nothing to do but go on with our last performances and spin every second out to its longest thread. We went to the hospital and gave the revue in our last wards, but try as we would, the days ran through our fingers.

We began to get bulletins from George Keane. We would have twenty-four hours in London before we started our journey home. This was something we had never dreamed of, and we tried to put our minds forward to it, instead of that inevitable last performance.

But it came, and we dressed and made-up, putting our things away as we were done with them, knowing we wouldn't take them out again, and we all listened behind the curtain as George Keane made his last introductory speech: "The American Theatre Wing in Association with the USO and Special Service takes very, very great pleasure in announcing the last performance of *The Barretts of Wimpole Street*."

"Perhaps it's true," said Brian, "but I don't think he needed to put in that extra 'very.' "

The curtain went up and "last" became a stencil. We heard our last whistles, our last cries of "pass it around," and McKay received his last hisses.

Off-stage Bill Noon defeated his last fireman and triumphed at last in French. Leaning against some derelict scenery, he lit his cigar, and the fireman pounced. He shook his finger in Bill's face and gave a superb imitation of scenery going up in flames. "Phffft!" he said to finish it off. Bill lit his Zippo lighter and ran it up the fireproofed curtains of Wimpole Street. "American scenery," he said. "*Pas* phffft!"

It was over. The men came back-stage and the company started packing. Nancy was putting the costumes into the wardrobe trunks, Keinert Wolff was collecting the make-up boxes and wigs. French stagehands came to crate the green sofa and the chairs, and Bob and Bill Noon were rolling up the liberated carpet. The walls of 50 Wimpole Street were down and Roger Stearns sat cross-legged on the stage untying them from their iron bars, and Kit and Brian still in their costumes were talking to one of the last GIs.

"And it's all true," Kit was saying; "this all really happened . . ." Beside me his friend was waiting, watching Kit as she talked. "That woman!" he said. "She's like a family reunion."

Later, when we were at the station waiting for the *rapide* that was to take us on the first lap of the journey home, Kit left us to walk up and down the platform alone, her hands deep in the pockets of her trenchcoat, her chin lifted above the turned-up collar. She walked with long fast steps, as though she were walking against the wind or time. A line of German prisoners passed her, as gray as the rubble they had created. Some of our own soldiers who were waiting went to her and she stopped. I saw her sign the programs they had saved, and then I saw her move abruptly away and continue to walk. The train came in, and we got aboard. Kit came back, her steps slower, and she was the last to get on. She sat near me and as we started she looked out of the window and the soldiers on the platform waved. She waved once, half in salute, then she sat back as if there was nothing more she could do.

"All right, Kit?" I asked her.

She nodded. "But up to the very last minute," she said, "I wanted the telephone to ring, and someone to ask us to stay."

CHAPTER SEVENTEEN

GEORGE KEANE counted us. "Sixteen," he said, "and when I count you on to the tender tomorrow that will be good-bye."

We had just left London. We were on the train for Glasgow and our port of embarkation. The train was full, and the B.O.W.S. were a tight fit in the three compartments allotted to them. There were no sleepers so we prepared ourselves to sit up all night.

I settled into a compartment with Bob and Bill Noon, Roger and Erik and Chester Stratton and Brian. Brian had his blanket neatly tucked around his legs, his knitted cap pulled over his ears, and he looked at me thoughtfully over his pipe. "My dear Watson," I expected him to say, but he didn't. Instead he said that he didn't think I ought to be in the compartment with all these men. I said that there were men in every compartment, there were just more in this one, and I preferred it.

"I can't sleep in a train, anyway," I said.

"Then don't talk," said Brian, "because I can."

Nancy came by and dropped a thin manuscript. "Something to read, Goldie."

I looked at the first page and read: "*In Savoy*, a play by Gertrude Stein."

"Miss Stein gave it to me, herself," said Nancy, "and I've discovered the secret of her style. Alice B. Toklas can't type."

I picked it up. There wasn't a punctuation mark to be seen.

"If you're going to read," said Brian, "turn the pages quietly."

There weren't many of them. The first act had only four, and ended petulantly: "Bah aristocrats make me wisk anything makes me wick everything"

Was that Miss Stein's spelling or Pussy's, I wondered. W is perilously close to S on a typewriter.

The lights were dim, and the compartment smelled of coal

and upholstery and leather and old tea-baskets, and the wheels clacked in the familiar rhythm of English trains. We half swayed, half joggled in time to it, and Miss Stein's words followed it faithfully:

CONSTANCE   I've just had a dreadful quarrel with Claude
            a really dreadful quarrel
HENRY   Did you well one does and one does and
            one does not but one mostly does did you

One *does* and one *does* and one *does* went the wheels. Brian put his pipe out and signified that he was turning in, but first he sighed. "I feel that our twenty-four hours in London was rather like the exit of the Demon King in a Christmas pantomime. A flash of light, a puff of smoke, and we were gone." He pulled his cap down and slept.

It had been exactly like that, I thought. From the moment our C-47 had landed us from France onto British soil to the moment our friends had seen us onto the train with a "God bless!" it had gone in a flash so bright that we had only a jumble of impressions to sort out later.

I leaned back against the smoky cushions and tried to separate mine. We had touched England. We had driven through Kent to reach London. We had moved like locusts to the telephones, but it had been Saturday and people were maddeningly out or away. We had reached the Lunts, and dashed to the theater where Laurence Olivier was playing. The last time we had seen him had been one New Year's just after he had married Vivien Leigh, and we had seen them off from America on a dismal ship in a downpour of rain. The blitz was at its height in London then, but he and Vivien wanted to be at home. The submarines were bad then, too, and I remembered wondering if they would ever get there.

Larry had been in the Air Corps; now he was out and acting again. The blitz was over, but there had been the V-1's and now the V-2's and we had heard their explosions almost at once. "You brought us luck, darling," said Lynn Fontanne when we left. "We have only had twelve since you've been here." That was one every two hours, but it made no difference to anyone. Business as usual. Danger was something to be endured but not dramatized. Everyone was in it together, everyone had the same chance one way or the other, so why talk about it?

"London is a foxhole," said Bob. "A great hospitable foxhole, and everybody shares it."

We saw the Lunts' play and we thought Lynn had never looked more beautiful, and that Alfred had never acted more truly. The audience was lavishly appreciative of them, with more than the usual link between actors and listeners; we felt there was the added bond of knowing that any moment might find them all in eternity together. But it was never in the open, and it didn't interfere with the ritual of tea trays that is part of a London matinee. They were still passed from hand to hand in the intermission and cups and saucers still rattled after the curtain went up on the next act. "Much more distracting than the bombs, darling," said Alfred.

Noel Coward used to say that success had a shine on it, and London had a shine on it, I thought, of courage and defiance and magnificent unconcern. The buttons who answered our bell at the hotel, the porter at the door, the maid who brought our breakfast, they were all the same.

"And it's raining, too!" the porter had said in disgust during a particularly heavy raid. The maid had begged me not to worry if a blast blew my clothes right off me and I found myself stark naked in the Strand. "It's only the concussion, dear," she said. "It can happen to anyone." But can everyone take it like that, I wondered. "One *does* and one *does* and one *does* and one *does*," went the wheels on the tracks.

I thought about the party that Clemence Dane had surprised us with, and the people we had met there. I had never known such warm friendliness, such wholehearted reaching out. They accepted us as if we had been with them through all their six years of endurance. They talked about the blitz and the bad blitz as if we would recognize the distinction. To me a blitz was a blitz, one as bad as another. They made a distinction in districts, too. Those that have been completely destroyed are the bombed districts; those only partially hit are not worth talking about.

We had time to see a little of the bad ones. There were only foundations left, but there was a difference in London's ruins. Italy and France had ruins of rubble and waste, barely cleared for passage way. London was neat, as if pride had scrubbed the bones of its skeleton clean.

It's a good foxhole, we thought as we left it; God bless!

The train was going faster and the wheels clacked round and round; we passed stations that were only black masses in the dark. I remembered when they were bright with lights and travel posters, when tours were many and varied. A third-class passage and the whole thing in thirty days, or first class and leisure, and money to spend in it. Paris, London, and Rome. The Beautiful Riviera, the Playground of the World. Stickers on a suitcase, stickers in your mind. Beaches and parasols, beaches and mines. "*Achtung Minen*" and *shü*-mines as thick as potatoes in a patch. The painted faces on the terrace at Cannes came back to me, and the thin ones of the young girls at the Officers' Club. Paris, London and Rome. Rome, beautiful, hungry, waiting, distrustful. See the Beauty of Italy. I could see the old poster, orange trees and brown faces and outrageously blue skies. Faces came crowding as we had seen them in Florence, white and anguished and afraid. Montecatini and the soldiers in the courtyard and the men in shabby black begging for work for bread alone. "We'll do anything—we'll work twenty-four hours a day—give us a tin of milk, a loaf of bread for it—anything." Children waiting at the kitchens for scraps from the soldiers' plates or slops from their mugs. Paris, London, and Rome. Paris was hungry, too, and lonely and suspicious. Paris, London, and Rome. The bombed districts of London and those not worth talking about. "You must see St. Paul's," Clemence Dane had said. "It stands alone as Christopher Wren conceived it, but in the spring crocuses come up to cover the devastation around it, and in the summer there are blankets and blankets of poppies." Paris, London, Rome. Every turn of the wheels was taking us further from them and closer to America. But America was in Europe, too, I thought. All over the face of it—supplies, ammunition, medicine, food, clothes, men. It was all one now. We were linked by lines of troops, and lines of stretchers, and lines of crosses. It should be a strong chain, I thought, it could be . . .

One *does* and one *does* and . . . one does *not* . . . but . . . one *mostly* does . . . the wheels were slower and we were pulling into Glasgow.

Brenda came to the carriage door with Flush under her arm. "I'm a little worried about Treasure," she said. "He got in and out of England all right, but there's a horrid rumor that he won't be allowed on the ship; they don't understand that he's one of the company."

I said I was sure it was all right, but if there was any trouble Gert would take a hand.

"Well," said Brenda, quivering, "I do hope so. Don't tremble, Music," she added to Flush. "If you stay, I stay."

We changed to the train that was to take us to the docks. An hour now and we would be on the tender, a few minutes after that on the ship. We wondered what it would be like, and wondering we began to feel that we were really on the way home. The tender, the ship, I thought, and then a taxi, and the elevator would be bringing me to my own door again.

We were on the tender, and Brenda was prepared for battle. On the train she had dressed Flush in a coat she had bought him in Paris and on it she had sewn his six months' overseas bar, the Ninth Army patch, and the Fifth Army patch. On his collar was his USO insignia and at his throat was the American Theatre Wing pin, and his dog tag, and in the pocket of his coat was a small lace handkerchief.

"Now," said Brenda, "no one can possibly take him for a civilian."

We drew near to our ship, its outlines tremendous in the gray morning. It was the *Queen Mary*. She was filled with wounded, George Keane told us, who had been taken aboard the day before. We were the last to go on. We went up the gangplank, and Brenda was immediately stopped.

"You can't take that dog on board," said an officer, and Gert rushed into action, and Brenda and Flush were passed on.

"It's all right," said Gert. "I explained he was an actor and a member of the company."

"What did he think Flush *was?*" said Brenda indignantly.

Gert hesitated, and broke it as gently as she could. "I'm afraid he thought he was a Yorkshire terrier," she said.

The last of us came on board. "Sixteen," said George Keane, and went back to the tender.

"Good-bye, B.O.W.S.," he called to us.

"Good-bye, George; dear, dear George," we called back.

The tender started and we looked past it to the lovely snow-covered hills of Scotland. This was the end; this was it, Greely, we thought. We leaned over the rail which was lined with the ambulatory wounded. Men in casts again, and on crutches and without sight. Our ship began to move, and a man with his medical tag fluttering from his empty trouser leg was saying over and over to himself: "I don't believe it, I don't believe it. Not till I see the Old Lady in the harbor holding that torch for me."

Scotland was a dimmer and dimmer outline. Nancy beside me said there was going to be a hurricane. Kit was looking beyond Scotland to Montecatini and Florence and Heerlen. Brian came and put his arm through hers.

Suddenly the loud-speaker startled us. "Hear this! Hear this! All officers and civilians report immediately in the lounge. All officers," it repeated. "All civilians."

"That's us," said Gert, and we turned and went inside.

SOS-NATOUSA SPECIAL SERVICE
IN COOPERATION WITH USO-CAMP SHOWS

AND

THE AMERICAN THEATER WING

PRESENTS

KATHARINE CORNELL AND BRIAN AHERNE

IN

THE BARRETTS
OF
WIMPOLE STREET
BY

RUDOLF BESIER

WITH

MARGALO GILLMORE - McKAY MORRIS
BRENDA FORBES

......

Staged by GUTHRIE McCLINTIC

CAST

(IN ORDER OF APPEARANCE)

Doctor Chambers	**Guthrie McClintic**
Elizabeth Barrett Moulton-Barrett	**Katharine Cornell**
Wilson	Brenda Forbes
Henrietta Moulton-Barrett	**Emily Lawrence**
Arabel Moulton-Barrett	**Margalo Gillmore**
Octavius Moulton-Barrett	**Eric Martin**
Alfred Moulton-Barrett	**Chester Stratton**
Charles Moulton-Barrett	**Robert Ross**
Henry Moulton-Barrett	**Roger Stearnes**
George Moulton-Barrett	**Reinert Wolff**
Edward Moulton-Barrett	**McKay Morris**
Bella Hedley	**Betty Brewer**
Henry Bevan	**Roger Stearnes**
Robert Browning	**Brian Aherne**
Doctor Ford-Waterlow	**Robert Ross**
Captain Surtees Cook	**Chester Stratton**
Flush	**By himself**

PRODUCTION STAFF

Stage Manager	Elaine Perry
Stage Technician	William Noon
Production Assistant	Nancy Hamilton
General Manager	Gertrude Macy

KATHARINE CORNELL

UNIT 319

First Row: Gertrude Macy, Betty Brewer, Brenda Forbes, Margalo Gillmore, Katharine Cornell

Second Row: Nancy Hamilton, Emily Lawrence, Elaine Perry, Brian Aherne

Third Row: Erik Martin, Guthrie McClintic, Chester Stratton, McKay Morris

Fourth Row: Roger Stearns, Robert Ross, Keinert Wolff

"CLIMBING DOWN THE RIGGIN'"

GAS HOUSE GANG
Brian, Kit, Margalo, McKay, Guthrie

Army Signal Corps

DANCE IN THE SUN

Army Signal Corps

"HAYFOOT, STRAWFOOT . . ."

BRIAN AHERNE

MCKAY MORRIS

Lieutenant George Keane

BRENDA FORBES

Vandamm

FLUSH GOES OUT WITH BRASS

"A ROOM WITH A VIEW" FROM KIT'S WINDOW IN FOGGIA

GENERAL MARK CLARK

Theatre at Foggia

Robert Ross

STAGING AREAS

Theatre at Bari

Robert Ross

Robert Ross

KIT'S FIRST FLIGHT—THE TAKE-OFF

Robert Ross

"FOR THE GOOD OF THE SEVENTEEN"

BOB AND MARGALO

WATCHING THE PLANE TURN OVER

Army Signal Co

MR. AND MRS. BROWNING WITH BRIAN AND KIT

Robert Ross

FAMILY OF THE BRIDE

Army Signal Corps

LIEUTENANT AND MRS. ROBERT HESTER

John Gerard

FLUSH

". . . as delicate as air . . . a lion in endurance."